MY SONG TO SING

MY SONG
TO SING

ADAM NICHOLAS BROCK

NEW DEGREE PRESS

My Song to Sing

My Song to Sing is a memoir about Adam Brock's personal development during adolescence and young adulthood. Every story uses facts, emotions, and memories to convey his understanding of the experiences that most define him. Brock occasionally modifies names, locations, details, and/or timelines for reasons of privacy or to guide this book's narrative.

ISBN
978-1-63676-360-6 *Paperback*
978-1-63676-443-6 *Kindle Ebook*
978-1-63676-363-7 *Digital Ebook*

For Kimberly, Steven, Desmond, Janice,
Richard, Anita, John, and Gia

And for Joan and Herbert, who live on in
the memories they helped create

CONTENTS

AUTHOR'S NOTE

Autumn leaves are a sublime feature of fall in Philadelphia. Their transformation from lively green providers of shade to the eventual crunch under my foot is as predictable as the season's change. I watch a few remaining leaves slowly descend in the coolness of November 2018 with knowledge that someday, on the right day, they will live a life beyond their original tree. These crinkled travelers know not where they're going but have the certainty that the wind at their backs is surely taking them *somewhere*.

"12:29 p.m., almost time," I mutter to myself as I inhale a deep, cleansing breath.

I draw away from a window in Temple University's Writing Center and prepare for a meeting with Dr. Barbara Gorka, Director of Temple's Fellowships Advising Office. I plop myself into a chair with only one question in mind: *What am I going to say?* My post-collegiate future waits just around the corner and I'm still stuck deciding what to do after graduation.

"Alright, Adam, you're free to come in," rings out from a nearby room.

I enter Barbara's office and we get right down to business.

"So," she asks, "what are your thoughts regarding the future? Are there any programs or positions that best fit your goals?"

I respond after a brief pause and another deep breath. We debated a variety of possible options, poking and prodding at research grants, graduate studies, and international opportunities between the mighty Rhine and the palaces of Vienna. While I knew my meeting with Barbara would be informative, I had no idea it would lead to my first book.

I am compelled to write a memoir because my journey through young adulthood was dominated by change. My plans after graduation were nothing like my expectations at the start of college; at first I was shocked, almost concerned that my situation had deviated too far from what I originally wanted to pursue after high school. Then again, after watching my goals and expectations shift over the past five years, I can confidently state I'm exactly where I want to be, maybe even supposed to be.

Becoming an author is one of the greatest transformations thus far in my life, and I must admit I'm still terrified of this project. I have never written something so personal about myself, family, or friends. Reading chapters out loud in my apartment is one thing, but sharing my thoughts with the internet and the whole wide world is probably the most vulnerable thing I've done in a long time, maybe ever. That's just it though. You never know exactly what life has in store for the future. My mother and father experienced that in their own stories and I'm just at the start of understanding mine.

There's an irony in my simultaneous support and evasion of change. It can be so convenient to get caught up in repetitive cycles of activities and expectations for weeks or months on end, so certain of what to expect from the future without any fear of deviation or surprise. Pete Seeger sings about this phenomenon in his song *Little Boxes*—how senseless conformity and resistance to change can, after enough time, turn us into a tiny package, lost in some factory warehouse, waiting to be snatched, opened, and dissected like every other one out there. Seeger speaks to the conveyor belt of life, an assembly line cluttered with prescribed courses of action regarding schools, careers, friends, and family. Following others' suggestions is not inherently unwise, and I know many individuals who found their calling after pursuing traditional career paths and doing everything they were advised to do. These standard recommendations are absolutely perfect for some but become problematic for others who shy away from change because they're told their ideas are not smart, not practical, not what *someone else* did.

What I find most important is the strength to welcome and enjoy change. I always considered myself to be on a consistent trajectory since middle school, and friends joke I've been the same person for as long as they can remember. However, I came to the conclusion after drafting this book that my path through young adulthood was always bending, always leading me away from the places I stood before.

Though I wrote this memoir to resonate with readers of all ages, I specifically designed my story for young adults, an audience going through the same transformative period I just navigated over the last ten years. Confronting uncertainty is a frightening task during young adulthood, but anyone can make advantageous decisions during this period by accepting uncertainty as a friend, not foe. I used the uncertainty and subsequent opportunities presented in the last ten years to make intentional choices for my future, completing my own tightrope walk between conformity and nonconformity. In keeping one foot on that traditional conveyor belt and the other on something new altogether, I charted my own course through the end of 2020.

I tackled challenges, expectations, and an uncertain future with my six tools for navigating change. They are the most useful lessons I acquired in young adulthood and were instrumental in helping me find my way through college. They pushed and pulled me from one activity to the next, nudging me to explore new places, meet amazing people, and embark on adventures around the world as I gradually discovered the man I am today. These ingredients for change populate the first six sections of my story and are individually highlighted in discussions of music performance, the world of ice hockey as a player and referee, my undergraduate experience at Temple University, excursions in Europe, and my ultimate acceptance of an English teaching fellowship in Austria. They became even more crucial for navigating the ongoing pandemic, the greatest life-altering event of our time that defines the word change.

I hope this memoir will help you reflect on your own experiences and plan a bright and promising future. You may not agree with my opinions. You may even reject my decisions and assumptions, but the cold hard truth is that I did my best to answer the same questions we all encounter in young adulthood. What you do with my story is up to you, but how you navigate change, and what you make of your life, might just belong in your own book.

Very truly yours,
Adam Nicholas Brock

In the race to be better or best,
miss not the joy of being.

ANONYMOUS

HIGH SCHOOL

BEGINNING OF IT ALL

Chris Rinaldi enters the activities fair with a look of dread. Another useless event means another waste of time. He struts with an orange Flyers T-shirt clearly displayed above a pair of shiny green basketball shorts. It's middle school in 2009: what else would you expect?

He takes a cautious first step onto the squeaky basketball court, mustering enough energy to peruse a few tables. Might as well pretend he's trying.

The gymnasium is filled to the brim with fancy decorative displays and chaotic clusters of sweaty sixth graders. Club and activity names run down Rinaldi's guidebook like the faint sweat trickling down the back of his neck: Science Olympiad, Chorus, Math Club. He looks up from the booklet and stares.

His disinterest is staggering.

Rinaldi begins his sacrificial circumvention of different stations with a gait indicative of little actual investment. One, two, three tables go by as the chatter only grows in volume with each passing group of students. He veers left to avoid a noisy crowd, following the path of as little social engagement as humanly possible, when a promising glimpse suddenly catches his eye. Rinaldi turns, points, stands still for only a second, and then makes a beeline toward a table with red, white, and blue decorations. He's attracted by more than just the shine of glittering cardboard cut-outs.

"Interested in playing ice hockey?" A kid stationed on the right side of the display speaks with a small smile and what must be an ice hockey jersey hanging below the waistline.

"Ah, what, ice hockey?" responds Rinaldi.

Wow, he thinks, *they have an ice hockey team? Nobody told me that. That's amazing! But, well, I know this kid. He looks too familiar.*

Rinaldi reaches aimlessly into the past, scavenging for any memories to connect this stranger at the booth with a pressing feeling of déjà vu.

This kid's definitely not from Conshy, not the bus, but I recognize the face...of that guy from chess club?

He looks once more at the kid.

Yeah...yes that guy from chess club. He's the first one I beat.

"You wanna play?" repeats once again.

Rinaldi clears his throat. "Could you tell me more about the team?"

"We're part of the Plymouth Whitemarsh Ice Hockey Club. Our program just restarted this year and I think there's a high school team. Do you play?"

Noise from other tables disappears as Rinaldi looks down, crossing both arms in front of his chest. "Yeah, actually. I rollerblade, you know...can go between the legs and shit."

The kid's eyes light up. "No kidding! Nice Flyers shirt by the way."

"Thanks, yeah I love the Flyers and hockey but never really ice skated before," says Rinaldi, now staring between his sneakers at the court lines below.

"That's okay, we have some other guys who just started. Maybe you could learn to skate with us."

"Hmm, maybe, I'm not sure." Rinaldi wipes his brow and takes an ice hockey pamphlet.

His eyes glow while scanning pages of stats, team pictures, and action shots. "Your club looks pretty cool and I always wanted to play, but I never tried anything like that before."

"Then you should play with us! I think you'll like it."

Is it really worth it? Rinaldi lingers at the table, quickly tapping one foot while intently examining the colorful paper.

Who knows how much this costs or what Mom will say. I might even suck at it. But, then again, this guy's pretty friendly. I think playing hockey would be really fun. What's the worst that could happen?

He looks up from the pamphlet.

"Yeah, I'll play."

***

When I talk to Chris Rinaldi today, we both still laugh over those first few moments in middle school, the beginning of what would soon become a long and enduring friendship. "You know," says Rinaldi, "at that time in my life, I maybe had about three friends and social anxiety. I remember being together in that chess club and would have never joined hockey without running into you at that activities fair."

The impact of our meeting lasted well beyond 2009 and Rinaldi knows as much: "I will always be grateful for that turning point, the conversation about playing hockey. It's one of those things where we were young and went with the flow, but now, I can still see how that event is affecting my life to this day. I wouldn't have gotten my hockey friends and family without it. A lot of my experiences are through hockey, including becoming captains together."

Some of the most crucial moments in life have humble beginnings. Many start with a question, the first assessment of one's conviction to complete a task, become a slightly new person, or take on unfamiliar and unforeseen challenges. In Rinaldi's case, all it took was a simple "You playing?" and his own personal drive to change his life as he knew it. Neither of us thought this moment would be a turning point. We were just some sweaty kids in middle school. Nevertheless, there's beauty to be found when looking back at our pasts, tracing decisions, reconstructing our hockey careers one piece at a time, and then finally finding the beginning of it all.

Turning points like Rinaldi's are critical junctions along the winding path through life. They have the power to shape decades, even lifetimes, and will ultimately bring one either closer or farther from where one stands today and seeks to go. The challenge for all people then becomes understanding how to make those impactful and intentional choices in real time. Danish philosopher Søren Kierkegaard once mused in his *Journalen* that "life can only be understood backwards, but it must be lived forwards." So how do we guide ourselves in the present, let alone make the correct choices for a future that is not yet understandable?

When reflecting on how I made the big decisions that guided me through the last several years, I realized my choices boiled down to a simple question about the future, one which was inspired by my friend Chirag Agarwal and our discussions about Christopher Nolan's *Inception*:

Am I prepared take a leap of faith on my ambitions?

Chris Rinaldi's decision to take a chance on ice hockey was his own leap of faith, a turning point which supported a love of sport and its community for years to come. He had so little to lose and so much to gain with this single activities fair decision. In choosing to fearlessly pursue a new opportunity with ice hockey and reject any lingering doubts about his choice, Rinaldi put himself on a path to continue playing hockey for years to come.

Rinaldi's story highlights my first key ingredient for navigating change: passion.

Passion brought Chris Rinaldi out of the crowd and delivered him to that activities fair table. Passion sustained his curiosity about a chance to play the sport he adored. Perhaps most importantly, it was following passion that subdued Rinaldi's fears and made him ready to step outside his comfort zone.

I offer no naive guarantee that everyone can discern their passions as easily as Rinaldi did in 2009. People are messy; they have many interests, conflicting priorities, and dreams that may not be understood until the latest stages of life. Be that as it may, the singular fact remains that passion is one of the most beneficial tools when taking a leap of faith (or two) and sticking to it.

These influential decisions may thrust you onto the conveyor belt of life or send you in a completely different direction, never to look back again. Regardless of where a leap of faith leads you, I insist that each and every choice in life, big or small, plays a crucial role in guiding us to the places we really want to go. Finding and utilizing passion, along with the other five lessons spread throughout my story, makes these decisions both easier and more relevant to your ultimate calling.

Nurturing my passions was one of the most influential aspects of my high school experiences. By fusing a love for ice hockey and music, I found common ground between seemingly incompatible activities that would further develop in later stages of young adulthood. The experiences and friendships I gained throughout public school then left me on the doorstep of a journey that fostered new passions, challenges, and leaps of faith like never before.

The upcoming adventure into my past highlights one of the many beauties in writing: the ability to immortalize moments in time. Points throughout my own history are preserved and cared for on these very pages. Literature possesses this singular and eternal duality, pairing resurrections of the past with simultaneous protection from the chaos of day-to-day events and the mundane punctuality of everyday life.

Let us enjoy Kierkegaard's concept of "living forward" while traveling backward in time to rediscover the meaning and truth in our personal histories, to search for motivations, successes, and shortcomings. It is then through the analysis of all those things which lie in the shadows that we will truly come to an understanding of ourselves, what decisions have guided us to our current condition, and how we plan for a prosperous future.

As such, I welcome you to the long expedition ahead. We will ascend the mountains, gaze over the valleys, and fight through the storms I've encountered in the last decade of my life. Our paths align today as we travel along mine together, preparing to discover ourselves on what can only be that voyage back in time through samplings of my journey.

THE ICE HAWKS

Ice hockey ruled my early teens. I fondly recall pulling my skate laces extra tight before the thrill of another game, another shift, and another chance to participate in the greatest sport on Earth for nearly ten years. There came a point toward the end of my playing career where appreciating ice hockey became a job in its own right, and my new duties as a referee added a degree of complexity to my relationship with organized sport. My role changed, but I continued on, nonetheless.

Though my vision fogs as I search for the first moments in my ice hockey career, the absence of my earliest games is readily replaced by memories from late middle school and high school. They're organized in my mind like a stack of postcards, laminated pictures accompanied by handwritten descriptions of my panting breath after a long shift, the familiar pain of a bruising shoulder check, and the sincere friendships formed with teammates on the ice.

There are a few select memories which free themselves from the pile. They stand apart from the others, etched into the stone of my subconscious. Such are stories of profound passion, relentless willpower, and love of sport.

And then, of course, there's Chris Rinaldi.

I skate with my teammates from the Ice Hawks in what might be the last meaningful game of our season. Rinaldi and I are now several years beyond that activities fair meeting, and our time together as teammates has only facilitated the development of a shared brain on the ice. To see where Rinaldi stands is one thing; to know where he goes is quite another.

Skaters circle the rink like bumper cars, moving from one crash to the next. Deep, jagged cuts litter the ice as passionate shouts erupt from each team over game strategies, seemingly uncalled penalties, and efforts to lower the temperature in what is an extremely heated affair. Tension over the outcome of this increasingly important contest splashes out of both benches, floods the ice, and spills into the bleachers where anxious groups of spectators fixate themselves on a black rubber disk.

The scoreboard taunts each and every Ice Hawk who dares to look upon it. Another season in early high school is winding down with each passing minute as only one singular goal separates us and our opponents from the playoffs. We have fought too hard and traveled too long throughout this past year to let an appearance in the post-season pass us by. The time is ripe to act if anyone has the will to do so.

"Alright boys, play's over!" asserts the referee after blasting his whistle.

I hit the brakes with my teammates in our defensive zone, pausing for much-needed rest in the finale to this wintertime rodeo. My gloves and stick hang wearily by my sides as I catch my breath and clear the fog in my head. I turn away from our goal crease for only a second, running through potential defensive scenarios before the impending faceoff, when a wrenching pain overwhelms my back. My whole body lurches forward, midsection before shoulders and torso. I hit the ground fast and hard, tumbling down like a rag doll. The ice is surprisingly cool and refreshing, seemingly undisturbed by the slight crackles formed from the impact of my gray helmet cage. As I turn my head to one side, still sprawled out on my stomach, I hear a raucous commotion ensue behind me.

Whistles blow, players shriek, and shouts erupt out of nowhere. Then comes another tremendous crash, like someone was rammed by a bus.

"Both of you off to the box!" demands one of the officials.

I tilt my head up slightly to see several players being separated and taken towards the penalty benches. No one's getting off easy this time.

"How 'bout you screw off bud?" chirps an opponent in what could have only been Rinaldi's direction. Here we go.

"Buddy, absolutely not. I just sent you *flying*. Go home," he responds without breaking a sweat. Rinaldi is no stranger to "chirping," the art form of trash-talking and riling up one's opponents.

"Pal, I get paid to play in this league. Look me up online," are the last few words I discern from our opponent as he and Rinaldi embark on their respective pilgrimages to the penalty box. This is by no means Rinaldi's first trip to the bench of shame, doubt it is for the other guy too.

But, come on, you get *paid* to play in this league?

Give me a break.

"Rinaldi, what the hell was that for, we just lost a power play!" are the first words to leave the mouth of Barry, our head coach. He stands with one foot on the bench and the other on the boards, leaning towards the ice with the urgency of a leader whose team's season is on the line.

Barry has a fair point. We did just lose a power play.

Rinaldi peeks his head over the penalty glass and addresses our team's bench. "Barry, Adam's our Captain. You dump him? I dump you. No exceptions."

He slams the penalty box door, tosses both gloves on the penalty bench, and bangs his stick against the wall. There are only a few minutes left, not much time to break through their defense and snag one more necessary goal.

The drawn-out fireworks after the illegal crosscheck to my back gave me enough time to collect myself, get back on my skates, and briefly discuss the upcoming situation with my teammates. We manage to maintain a strong defensive posture after resuming play, fighting for every loose puck and new opportunity during Rinaldi's two long minutes of detainment.

He bursts out of the box at the first whistle after his coincidental penalty. We gather our best forces with just a minute remaining, bringing out the top offensive and defensive lines as the referees prepare for another faceoff. The puck lands firmly on the ice as the clock begins its gradual decline to fifty-nine, fifty-eight, fifty-seven seconds.

Time to make our final push.

Defense up, goalie out, wingers crash the net.

Everything goes.

We regain possession of the puck and transition toward our opponents. I receive a firm pass from my defensive partner and charge forward, entering the left side of the offensive zone with Rinaldi and others spread out on my right. I make a quick stop, digging my metal skate blades deep into the frigid ice, and launch a large cloud of snow into the air. My gear suddenly triples in weight as I survey the entire scene.

Almost everyone is covered. Thirty-two seconds.

We've got to get this on net, but who's open? Well, Rinaldi's coming around from behind the near defender. He might just be our best shot.

I take a sharp turn, shift my balance to steer around an opponent, and complete a backhand pass to Rinaldi, knowing just where he'll be by the time the puck reaches his stick. He's positioned just above the goal line, working with options perhaps more limited than mine were. Eleven seconds.

Rinaldi looks, fakes, looks again. He strides forward, moves around a defender, and forces his way into the slot. His stick flexes back as he lets off a laser of a shot, flinging the puck with all the grit and emotion of a man destined to squeak out just one more goal. I instinctively skate toward the net after making the pass, because when all else fails, the least I can do is go where the puck should be.

Events begin to slow down in the final seconds. My eyes follow the puck from the blade of Rinaldi's stick as it cruises along the frictionless ice, evades two players, enters the dark blue paint of the goal crease, and approaches two rectangular goalie pads being urgently thrusted down onto the ice. I lose sight of the puck when it disappears under the goalie's jet-black equipment and peer around the other side of the goal in hope, desperate hope, for its much-needed reappearance.

One second passes, then another. It seems as if the universe has stopped its eternal motion in this singular moment. Every noise in the rink has seemingly vanished as all eyes focus on Rinaldi's shot in these last few seconds.

Out of the vacuous darkness in between the goalie pads comes a shadow and then the black, circular mass of its creator. It remains steadfast in trajectory, apparently committed to reach the end of some epic marathon.

The puck wiggles out from behind the goalie and maneuvers across the goal line. I look up slowly from the net, noticing the return of all sound and energy to the building.

The referee points for a good goal. Two seconds.

***

My passion for ice hockey was not born but rather grew out of moments where my teammates and I put it all on the line for the game we loved. Few things build character more effectively than literal experience, whether that's on the ice or in any other activity that fosters camaraderie and strengthens relationships.

No one can ever take away this game from Rinaldi and me. Histories like this one with the Ice Hawks do not cease to be simply because the action itself has passed. The memories of that final goal and our subsequent embrace will always exist, tucked away beside numerous ice hockey postcards in the depths of my mind.

The friendships I developed with teammates like Rinaldi were some of the greatest gifts I received from playing ice hockey. I've seen that same last-second goal scorer many times at the beach, the bar, and with the others who made the Ice Hawks a second family during my teenage years. It was as if Rinaldi and I found ourselves on the same path, one which led to a passion for ice hockey until our legs gave way at some date and time which I cared not to fathom. We were young and playing the sport of our lives. *What more could we ask for?*

What did surprise me about my passion for this game is how it could, under the right circumstances, entirely unravel. Experience enough would eventually prove how ice hockey, a sport which seemed so innocent in my mind as a young high school student, had a far darker potential.

THE HUSKIES

War has plagued mankind since antiquity. Too often have we fought and too soon do we seek to fight again.

American writer Randolph Bourne once asserted in *The State* that "war is the health of the state," the means for man's persistence. Despite all human progress over the last few centuries, I sometimes wonder if he was right that the state depends on conflict to hold itself together.

I never expected to find a parallel between Bourne's statement and my passion for ice hockey during high school. Most memories from my playing days are based in beauty, artifacts enshrined in a golden hue. However, when searching deep into my memory banks, rediscovering ancient manuscripts hidden in the mustiest corners of the bookshelf I call my head, I uncover a sinister past to the game I thought I knew. The only question remaining is if it had to be this way.

Chris Rinaldi strides into the offensive zone on what looks to be a breakaway. Beating two defenders and sliding past a winger, he crosses the blue line and begins a final dash to the goal. He fixates himself on another strategic success, craving that sensation of propelling the puck past the opposing goalkeeper into frayed, grungy lacing on a rusty iron frame. Each powerful stride digs Rinaldi deeper into the shell-shocked ice, moving him one step closer to achieving utter, if not inevitable, destruction of his opponents.

He and I are members of a team called "The Huskies" in a different season from that buzzer-beating game with the Ice Hawks. Nothing but bad blood had been boiling between us and our current opponents since our very first game, and we're facing off today in the championship. All our forces assemble together on this game for the ages and are hell-bent on dominating the competition. After a season-long struggle against a well-studied foe, one fact about today's game is abundantly clear: the pressure cooker of our rivalry is ready to explode.

We find ourselves on the way to victory in the final minutes of the 3rd period. Every Husky has sloshed through the muck of battle, pursued every opportunity to quash the enemy with unyielding zeal. Rinaldi, the clever general of our Huskies, knows the opponents' chances for victory are dwindling by the second. He strides into the offensive zone not simply to fatten our commanding lead, but rather to smash their window of opportunity into a thousand pieces.

Rinaldi doesn't just crave another goal. He needs it.

A flash of light suddenly shines out of the corner of his eye. He quickly looks back to find none other than his archrival, an enemy commander who has pestered Rinaldi since their first shift together. Hairs on the back of his neck stand up as a final clash between tribal leaders is almost inevitable.

The ice vibrates under their combined strides towards the goal crease like the ground trembled under all those armies and warriors of old. Rinaldi's challenger takes a ravenous leap and digs into the back of his left shoulder. Rinaldi fails to fight off the attack and stumbles with his delirious opponent. They fall together like mortar shells, detonating on impact and sending ice crystals radially outward from their collision.

"You're done buddy, get ready to eat shit!" screeches the rival, the degree of his insane obsession to instigate this clash of titans only now becoming apparent. Rinaldi turns, lays his stick down, and then gets on one knee before grabbing his combatant.

There is often a tipping point in the greatest of battles, one which turns the tide in an epic struggle. Like Pickett's Charge in the fields of Gettysburg, the finale of today's conflict would prove disastrous for the aggressor.

The two wrestle to the ground and begin a standoff for the ages. One strike, then another. Rinaldi lands a third jab underneath the helmet strap. The building trembles as all players, fans, and rink staff spectate the ongoing conflict. Three more successive hits leave Rinaldi's adversary dazed and confused, struggling to land the simplest of blows. Rinaldi finishes his initial siege with the ferocity of a rabies-infected animal.

Both officials finally arrive on scene. "Don't take the helmet off, I'm telling you, don't do it!"

Like that would make a difference to the guy I met in chess club.

Rinaldi grabs the opponent's cage with a surge of adrenaline, dismembers the helmet straps, and destroys all bolted connections. He then rips off the helmet and tosses it aside to expose the maniacal grin of his bruised adversary. The opponent is still committed to the madness he started throughout the entire beat-down, seeking a victory that was never to be had.

Gloves, sticks, a helmet. They litter the ice as Rinaldi's confrontation sparks minor clashes between other players. I skate up from our defensive zone to observe the whole scene, taken back by the chaos of this newly formed no man's land.

The main fight is surrounded by other small skirmishes as players from both benches yap and howl like wild animals, energized by the chaos unfolding before them. Each coach tries to calm his team as spectators begin reflecting on the mayhem presented before them.

Jesus Christ, I think to myself, *this really is hell.*

It takes all the effort of both officials to eventually separate Rinaldi from his hopeless challenger. Still retaining that deranged smile, he cusses at Rinaldi and the rest of us while flipping off the crowd for good measure. The clock ran out near the beginning of their struggle and officially secured our victory.

Rinaldi directs his own path off the ice, hardly held back by the struggling referees. Gazing up towards the stands, he sees an irate figure banging the glass who could only be a parent of his unhinged opponent.

"Hey!" he shouts. "Your kid is a punk!"

Each team assembles together and follows behind its (in)famous combatants as they leave the ice through opposite doors.

"You guys want round two? Won't be so lucky next time!" echoes from across the hallway.

"I kicked your asses once and I'll whup 'em again!" chirps back Rinaldi.

The true festivities begin after the Huskies gather in their locker room. There's no shortage of compliments for today's hero.

"Nice job Rinaldi, way to go!"

"Yeah, we trashed that team. Talk about a bunch of dicks."

"Rinaldi, man, that was brutal! You really messed 'em up!"

The compliments keep pouring in as I look around at my teammates and consider the price of our conquest. We fought through each and every minute of that championship game and overpowered our nemeses in the most brutal way possible. Immediate reflection after events of such magnitude is never fully complete and often tainted by excess emotion. Nevertheless, I stand transfixed from a nagging thought in the back of my mind as my teammates indulge themselves in our conquest, drunk on the spoils of victory.

Here we are, a band of brothers united by our commitment to each other and this great game. We win and lose as one, each member giving himself up for the whole on the front lines of battle. The Huskies engage in combat with an unwavering commitment to our teammates and the "greater good," or so we prefer to think.

Our casualties are extremely light, nothing like the ultimate and life-changing sacrifices made in real war. Though our physical losses may be insignificant, I fear that the spirit of this championship game, and perhaps the intentions of ice hockey as a whole, suffer greatly from conflicts such as today's. We won our battle after demonizing our opponents, exploiting suppressed energy, and demanding punishment of our adversaries.

The question resurfaces. Did it *really* have to be this way?

Youth sports helped me build many friendships, discover new things about myself, and develop my passion for ice hockey. However, they also promote a pervasive idea of otherness. In degrading our opponents to nothing more than "the enemy" in games such as this championship, we foster that *us* versus *them* mentality, a mindset that is arguably at the root of human conflicts throughout the ages.

Religion, politics, war: it's always *us* and *them*. As I stand among my teammates, I wonder if extreme competition and the denigration of opponents are parts of a spirited youth activity or means to develop rivalries focused on fighting, hatred, and vengeful passion. Does this seemingly well-intentioned goal to unite our tribe serve the greater good of our game, or does it rather confirm Bourne's suspicions that "war is the health" of our sport?

Physicality and aggression will always be parts of ice hockey, and to stand up for teammates as Rinaldi did in the previous chapter is one of the many positive lessons learned from organized sports. However, it seems that game participants too often lose sight of why they're really involved with competitions like that fateful Huskies championship in the first place. A state-like group mentality, rather than cherishing the joy of athletics and teamwork, encourages and practically condones extreme polarization between opposing forces.

Just as sports bring us together, they can also rip us apart.

I have no regrets about my love of ice hockey but am acutely aware that the sport suffers from self-inflicted wounds. It was after games like this championship with the Huskies that I began to explore other interests outside the ice rink. Embracing a full-time hockey schedule throughout my adolescence, a choice eagerly made by many of my teammates and friends in high school, was just not a commitment I could make. The time was right for pursuing a new passion.

"Hey, Brock. Brock!" creeps out from somewhere behind me.

Thoughts of tomorrow only carry me so far from the actions of today. My back slumps as I slowly pivot in the direction of my teammates.

"You good? C'mon, we're getting a group photo."

Several waves usher me over to the other side of the room.

"Yeah, I'm fine," I mutter while taking a few steps backward to join the crowd.

NUMBER TWENTY-FIVE

We're taught from an early age to reject failure at all costs. Run, dodge, duck—don't let it hit you. Aim for the sky because the ground ain't got nothin' on it.

After moving beyond that Huskies game in search of something new, I decided to make a serious investment in my passion for music. The arts have always been a part of my life, and I have many fond memories of attending music school before kindergarten and singing with my mom and brother during long car rides. She likes to recall instances from the early 2000's when my brother and I sang along to cassette tapes on our front porch, tuning our high-pitched voices to songs I can only dream of now. Ten years later, my brother and I moved on from those cassettes to pursue clarinet and saxophone performance throughout middle and high school.

Music was an ever-present passion in my early teens that hardly led to failure. I certainly encountered difficulties at one point or another, but often found myself feeling quite comfortable, even somewhat arrogant, with my abilities as a young clarinet player.

My overconfidence only lasted for so long. To this day, I am forever thankful for my involvement with competitive music performance. Music competitions, along with their entrance auditions, significantly challenged my beliefs about achieving success during high school.

There was once a young clarinetist who decided to take on the world. Years of participation in school music ensembles and local honor bands left him craving something more, a new occasion to flex his muscles as a high school sophomore.

Participation in Pennsylvania Music Educators Association (PMEA) events seemed to be the most promising opportunity. Every year, PMEA hosts a series of competitive music auditions and concert festivals across the state for motivated high school musicians. They start at the district level and then progress to regional and all-state ensembles. District auditions usually occur sometime in early December, and the best musicians from each district are invited to play in concert bands, orchestras, and choirs during the first few months of the following year.

The young clarinetist decides that these festivals are for him and eagerly approaches PMEA auditions for the first time in December 2013. He needs to place within the top twenty-four clarinets in District 11, an area demarcated by Bucks and Montgomery counties, to qualify for the District 11 Concert Band.

This district has a reputation for being one of the most competitive battlegrounds in the state. As such, he spent the last few months preparing for the challenge. He practiced his scales, learned excerpts from Mozart's *Clarinet Concerto*, and completed an occasional sight-reading exercise for good measure. He would be evaluated on all three of these criteria and was more than satisfied, even arrogant, about his preparation for district auditions.

The clarinetist arrives early at Central Bucks East high school on the audition day in early December. It's not exactly clear how his scales, excerpts, and sight-reading will be assessed, but this is of no matter. He's done the job, put in the work, and earned the right to play in PMEA ensembles.

His moment of truth arrives sooner than expected. All district auditions are split into three separate evaluations, and the portions concerning scales and the *Clarinet Concerto* occur with almost no issues.

Just one more part, dashes through his mind while he prepares for the sight-reading segment. *Time to finish the job. Nice and easy.*

He struts into the sight-reading room and is greeted by a music educator. One lonely piece of sheet music sits upside down on a music stand, imitating some valuable treasure like the one found in the opening scene of Steven Spielberg's *Raiders of the Lost Ark.* What remains to be seen is if it comes with all the necessary booby-traps and life-or-death scenarios.

The door closes swiftly behind him as the educator explains how the clarinetist has thirty seconds to analyze this piece. He will then play on command and exit thereafter. Three judges sit silently on the far side of the room with their backs facing toward him.

He nods his understanding and she flips the blank page to reveal a short passage only four staff lines in length. The young musician starts analyzing the work after she starts her timer. He notes the key, tempo, and all challenging rhythms before looking up at the wall clock.

His thirty seconds disappear much faster than he expected. Sweat starts to form in between the pads of his fingers and the silver-coated keys of his wooden clarinet. His instrument suddenly gains weight, resembling something closer to a tuba as the musical passage morphs into a single, indiscernible mass. He looks frantically down at the second line, then forgets the first, reads it again, now down to the third, but needs to check the second again, but wait, what even is the fourth line? Tick-tock.

His ears perk up at the sound of something even worse than his silent panic.

"Alright, that's time. Begin."

The young clarinetist lifts his massive instrument and does as instructed.

It's 3/4 time, he thinks, *let's get in the groove.*

A few measures pass by without issue. Then comes the dastardly E#.

E#...damn! Wait, that's F natural, I used the wrong fingering, no!

There's nothing like the classic harmonic struggle between an E# and F natural to trip him up in the most consequential audition of his life. He stutters through the following lines while his greasy fingers slip over tone holes on his instrument. Musical time ebbs and flows as he pulls back with every mistake and then rushes forward to counteract his own inconsistencies. Missed notes, improper articulations, no melodic phrasing, even wrong pitches. The young clarinetist had it all, until he didn't. Robbed by his own nerves and a childish mistake.

His final note is met by deflating silence. The educator glances over at the clarinetist, cold as ice, and indicates that he may now leave the room. He turns away, too shy to show her his puppy-dog eyes, and exits, leaving the door open behind him. The next performer enters as he sulkily retreats down the hall.

Audition results come back within a day. A student from another school sends him the placement list and he scrolls fervently through the PDF of over seventy-five clarinetists. All he needs is his name within the top twenty-four.

It's not number one, in the top five, or even near the top ten. He searches frantically—where could it be?

His eyes slam shut upon discovery.
Number twenty-five.

***

Fluke, mishap, defeat. Maybe just failure. Acknowledging mistakes is challenging enough. Even harder for the young clarinetist is coming to terms with them.

A few sluggish strides carry him to the front door of his private teacher's house. It's his first lesson since PMEA auditions and he winces with each knock on the front door, tail between his legs, embarrassment building up inside. Nathan Snyder greets him with the expected question.

"How did the audition go? I didn't hear anything about the results."

The clarinetist looks up, slowly unpacking his instrument.

"I did all I could but didn't make it. Was only one seat out, number twenty-five. I reached the end of my audition to only tank the sight-reading. I let us both down."

"I'm sorry to hear," replies Nathan, first looking at his distressed student and then down at the floor. He paces over to a pile of sheet music and carefully assembles the materials for today's lesson.

"But," he says, "what are you going to do about it?"

The clarinetist stops unpacking. "What do you mean? There's nothing more to do. I failed."

Nathan walks back and places a lesson book on the music stand.

"Well, it seems you have a choice to make. We can give up and stop working to improve for next year's auditions, or let this brief setback serve as motivation to push harder than ever before."

"But I put it all on the line this year, did everything possible to prepare," protests the young clarinetist. "I was so sure things were going to work out and no one is more responsible for this mistake than me. How can I go back out there? What more can I do?"

"It's simple," counters Nathan. "We need to raise the bar even higher. More practice, more sight-reading, more music. We can go there, maybe even get you to the top of those twenty-four spots, but that requires more than the necessary work. We need a whole new set of expectations. This year's failure can be a steppingstone to next year's success."

The clarinetist pauses, astounded by the idea that embracing this failure could be exactly what he needs to succeed. Nathan is offering an opportunity to actually make something out of his anguish if he has the guts to do so.

He pauses, looks down at his instrument, and then back up to Nathan.

"Seems like there's only one real choice. Let's do it."

***

I hardly expected failure to be one of my best teachers in high school. My experiences up through my mid-teens were relatively free of this taboo idea, the thought that I might not succeed at something because my pursuits, regardless of what they were, had to be successful. I was fully conscious of my interest in rejecting failure, be it out of an extreme case of perfectionism or the fear of experiencing seemingly dire consequences. My studies and activities went by without much struggle and I intended to keep it that way. Then came my 2013 PMEA audition.

What I did not realize about starting a serious investment in the arts is that it would inevitably lead to failure. No matter how great I thought I was, there were always going to be better players, harder pieces, and tougher auditions than I wanted to admit. My first PMEA audition and subsequent lesson with Nathan were a turning point in my musical career. I no longer wanted to be a young clarinetist who resisted failure. I needed to change my perspective about music, abandon my ego, and learn how to deal with situations when life doesn't go exactly as planned.

It took much more than a moment's decision to completely change my musical approach and goals. I sometimes asked myself in the months after my first audition if taking another chance on PMEA was still worth it. Music was always a part of my life, but was I truly ready to sacrifice more opportunities with hockey for a concert series that required so much time and effort?

My answer then, and certainly now, is absolutely. Though my passions for hockey and music were an uncommon pairing, I rejected any preconceived notion that they were incompatible activities. I sustained my interest in hockey with Rinaldi and other friends at the rink while nurturing my passion for music with a second PMEA audition.

The struggles from my first audition also led to a turning point in my academic life. I used that singular failure to improve my work ethic and investment in high school academics, college preparation, and even my post-collegiate future. I learned, and in this case the hard way, that we need to fail, and fail hard. Few things foster more discipline, encourage intentional behaviors, and develop real commitment like a slap in the face from struggles and challenges.

The longer we hide from failure, the longer we separate ourselves from all the productive motivation it has to offer.

I trained for my second PMEA audition with a drive to push harder than ever before. I began my second attempt in the late spring of 2014 and quickly purchased all the necessary music upon its release. Then came rigorous preparation for more than half of a year.

My practice routines were intense and intentional. Week after week of etudes, scales, and repetition of the same four page solo dominated much of my summer. Thirty minutes here, another hour there; I drove my scales, solo excerpts, and some sight-reading pieces so hard into my fingers that even today I can practice most melodies on a steering wheel, my leg, wherever. I pawned random music off the internet, found old manuscripts, and borrowed sight-reading books from Nathan. An endless number of reeds covered the floor around my music stand as three, four, even five days of practice per week became not the exception but the norm. I fought through the swollen lips and aching fingers, for my level of performance had to break all expectations and surpass any previous notions of success.

The investment in my second audition did not come without a price. PMEA preparation was my heartbeat from May to December, and hours of practice took away opportunities to spend time elsewhere with family or friends. When the work was at its toughest and I wanted to quit my PMEA journey, I kept Nathan in the back of my mind. My first audition and love of music were my motivation to improve my musical skills like never before. There was purpose in my suffering: I craved both the PMEA experience and the chance to overcome my fear of failing again. I enjoyed the months of work, both for their musical successes and challenges, and sought to prove once and for all that failure would be, in Nathan's words, the steppingstone to next year's success.

And just like that, as if my preparation was nothing more than a long day's work, I find myself back in Central Bucks East at the end of 2014. Another walk down the same long hallway brings me to the audition room with my clarinet in one hand and Cavallini's *Adagio and Tarantella* in the other. Each step lands firmly on the dark tile floor as I approach my chance for redemption with PMEA sight-reading.

A music educator greets me at the entrance to the sight-reading room and repeats the procedure for a process I know all too well. I walk in slowly and find another piece of music turned upside down after the door closes swiftly behind me.

SOMEWHERE CLOSE TO THE RAIN

"Alright everyone, let's take five."

Brian Balmages lowers his baton onto the conductor's stand and steps off the podium. He leans backward, stretching after another long chunk of rehearsal, and proceeds off stage.

Musicians set down their instruments and prepare for the much-needed break. I rise from my seat and exit the clarinet section as my lips immediately express their satisfaction with some temporary rest. The flood gates are lifted as students fill the Central Dauphin High School auditorium and dodge an assortment of instrument cases, music folders, and half-eaten granola bars scattered throughout the room.

Welcome to the 2015 PMEA All-State Band. My second PMEA audition was nothing like the first, and I was beyond fortunate to place fifth overall in those top twenty-four clarinetists and perform in the 2015 District 11 Band.

My transition from ice hockey to an investment in competitive music performance had finally paid off. This change in direction was not prescribed, was not part of the typical path through high school sports and music. Many friends and colleagues from both arenas could not and would not understand my interest in one activity or the other, thinking that anything besides a singular focus on one passion would blow up in my face. I was not the first to make such a transition in high school and will certainly not be the last. Too often does it seem that external expectations of conformity stunt such moves, preventing individuals from making the change they want to achieve.

Let this story be a reminder of the power found in pursuing passions. Better yet, of the rewards derived from failure.

Thankfully, this second audition was not the last stop in my PMEA journey. I participated in three festivals during early 2015: District 11 Band, District 11 Orchestra, and Region 6 Band, which pulls students from the entire Philadelphia area. Then, in the natural progression after Region Band, I qualified for the 2015 All-State Concert Band.

Musicians from every corner of the Keystone State gathered in Hershey, PA with one goal in mind: making amazing music. We've cast ourselves out to sea on a four-day musical quest with Brian Balmages at the helm of our ship. A renowned conductor and composer based out of Baltimore, Balmages was hired as the All-State Band director to offer guidance on the musical journey through life and share his perspective on the career of a professional musician. He's a man of medium height and slender build, whirling his baton with the passion of someone whose creed is music.

Balmages calls us back on stage after ten minutes.

"Let's get back to the de Meij. Measure, ahm, yes the clarinet introduction to the second theme."

Perhaps one of my most favorite pieces for concert band, Johan de Meij's *Symphony No. 1 "The Lord of the Rings"* captures Tolkien's epic saga in a unique musical texture. The All-State band is playing *Gandalf (The Wizard)*, the first movement in de Meij's *Symphony*. It is a bombastic work filled with waves of rich brass crashing against a shoreline of soft woodwind passages. The first theme is started by the bassoons, a special feature for an instrument that often lacks the melody in a concert band setting.

Balmages directs us to jagged clarinet lines that rip through murmurs from a dark percussion backdrop. The flick of his slim wooden baton is matched by twenty-four clarinets in the ready position. Our entire band lurches forward and begins describing what I can only imagine as Gandalf running through a cave, battling some orcs, or encountering a long-time foe like Saruman.

I look up after a few lines to notice Balmages becoming noticeably distracted and staring off into space. The crisp cuts and twirls of his baton lose momentum by the second. We begin to wobble as he lets go of the steering wheel to the sports car that is this ensemble, slowly edging us to the sides of a metrical road as different instruments begin falling out of time.

Balmages finally stops conducting and steps back, grabbing his head. He rests his baton on the conductor's stand and leaves the stage.

"Hold on, I'm sorry," he says while stepping away, "but I have to get this out of my head."

I look across the aisle to other musicians who share my confusion as he finds his way to a grand piano in the auditorium pit. Balmages quickly opens the cover and pulls up the bench. The room grows silent as he carefully leans forward and makes first contact with the keys.

Gentle whispers rise out of the stillness in the auditorium. He begins playing what I can only describe as a conversation between himself, the All-State Band, and nature. Balmages makes the keys work for him, telling stories of love and loss amid a backdrop of light, audible rainfall on the roof. Our maestro rocks and sways as his soft, non-metrical prose sweeps us up out of our seats into a world between the song and rain, a ballad tying together two different elements of nature.

I sit in my seat, motionless. All concerns about the piece at hand, All-State Band, high school, and my future just vanish. Balmages guides us out of the tangible world into something less physical but all the more real. Melodies tumble out from those black and white keys as I stare up at the ceiling. His notes populate the dry auditorium air, drifting up somewhere close to the rain but never quite touching it.

The piano eventually dulls to the sound of diminishing rainfall. Balmages decelerates his hands until they fall on the keys no more, subtly retreating into a silence that leaves the auditorium naked. We sit and stare in the beautiful pause that comes after any great song. It's in this temporary stillness, the second or two between the end of a performance and what would normally be applause, that the magic truly happens.

Balmages' notes fade away as purposely as his most powerful passages soared. He climbs back on stage, wipes some sweat off the brow, and readjusts his pair of thin glasses.

"Sorry everybody, I kept hearing that with the rain and couldn't focus on our rehearsal. Now, where were we?"

I pick up my clarinet in disbelief. My stand partner sits silently and flutists across the stage stare at Balmages with wide eyes and open mouths. Not even the percussion manages a peep. His question is met with virtual silence, nothing but the reserved applause of rain drops up above.

What seemed like a normal night at All-State band just took a turn for the extraordinary. I witnessed the ultimate grace and beauty of music, true genius, and improvised expression. Balmages provided insight into what the arts and improvisation are really all about. He charmed us in a shared language like I had never been spoken to before, conjuring abstract ideas with the keys under his fingers.

For perhaps the first time ever in the history of education, I like to think that this musical lecture was well received and digested by every single student in attendance. I may never again witness a lesson of the same magnitude, but if I know one thing for sure, it's that this magic happened once and will happen again. The power of music lives on, just waiting to be played and heard.

We resume rehearsal as rain keeps pattering on the roof of Central Dauphin High.

***

The words, or rather sounds, of Brian Balmages ring in my ears as I adjust my bow tie for what must be the thousandth time. I unpack my clarinet in the stuffy basement of the Hershey Theater and join my fellow musicians on stage.

We will soon showcase our musical growth after half a week of practice and rehearsal. Our black cushioned seats are aligned just so as nearly one hundred high school students from all over Pennsylvania sporadically populate their respective instrumental sections. An upward look to the ceiling and out toward the upper walls reveals magnificent tapestry and engravings, a collection of different murals that tell tales of old in this small concert hall.

Bits of chatter from parents and music educators drift out of the crowd as we begin rudimentary warm-ups. Today's performance will ideally be less improvised but contain all the same emotion and expression from our conductor's piano solo just days before.

Brian Balmages ascends the stage with a thoughtful expression. His glasses are clean, not a smudge to be found. He wears an all-black outfit with his hair parted just so.

Balmages greets us and addresses a series of logistical matters: cues, cutoffs, bowing, solo recognition. Just when it seems he's finished with any normal pre-concert speech, Balmages turns his focus to the future.

He leans both hands forward on the podium with a calming intensity.

"You know," he begins, looking around the ensemble, "someone is going to be the next principal horn of the Chicago Symphony. You need to decide if it's going to be you. Everyone here is incredibly talented and you've all worked hard to make it onto this stage. You have the power to transform your talent and passion into your dreams, both with music and anything else. All I ask is that you remember who *you* are and do what *you* want with your life."

Balmages leans back, nodding while we silently absorb his message, and grins. "Alright, let's make some music!"

Now I'm the one to smile. I never dreamed that my decision to pursue PMEA less than two years ago would lead to participation in multiple festivals, let alone Balmages' performance at the 2015 All-State Band. But a career in music? Despite all my involvement with the arts both at home and with PMEA, the thought of going all-in on studying music never crossed my mind until this passionate speech from one of the best in the business.

My original goal was balancing two passions, hockey and music, nothing more. But now, in the conclusion to my first year in the PMEA circuit, Balmages pops the big question. With college applications looming in the coming summer, I have to ask myself if I'm ready for another change in trajectory, a deviation grander than my move from sports to music.

While the future beckons with questions not yet ready to be answered, I have more important tasks at hand. The curtain rises and Balmages instructs us to rise from our seats in front of a packed house. He accepts the applause and turns back to face us.

Students sit down and prepare their instruments. I hold my clarinet at the ready, waiting for Balmages' signal. The concert begins with a flick of his baton and one large, collective breath.

THE ONE CALLED SIMONS

History has fascinated me since my early teens. The characterization of different periods by their timelines and relative importance to other events still intrigues me to this day, as the means of categorization alters my perception of the past.

Take the span from 1910 to 1940 in the United States. Within this thirty year period, the avid historian encounters the Progressive Era, the First World War, Prohibition, the Big Band Era, the Suffragettes, the revival of the Ku Klux Klan, the Great Depression, and so on. Yet when I think of one year in particular, say 1930, how exactly should I define this specific link in the American chain? Is this the first year of economic turmoil after the Crash of 1929, or rather the ten year anniversary of the Nineteenth Amendment and women's right to vote? Was this five years after the KKK marched on Washington DC or five years before the beginning of the Big Band Era?

It could be all, or maybe none. I'm no authority to decide. In my case, I can say with certainty that the period from 2013 to 2016 was the era of PMEA. I traveled from a failed audition in 2013 to a second All-States festival in 2016, tracing an arc through what was perhaps the most musically active period in my life.

The culmination my PMEA journey was unquestionably defined during the young months of 2016. It came after the final summer during high school, college applications, senior classes, my first last day of school. My third PMEA audition yielded results similar to those from the second, propelling me to both Region 6 Band and Region 6 Orchestra before clinching my final reunion with the 2016 All-State Band.

I had already committed to attending Temple University in the fall of 2016, and as the next chapter in my life inched closer with each passing day, I occasionally mused about a full-time investment in music. My final six months at Plymouth Whitemarsh High seemed to have a concert almost every two weeks and my musical chops were at their very best.

Despite my active music schedule, I nevertheless remained focused on my academic pursuits like physics, calculus, and English. Music, like my hockey schedule, remained a passion I separated from the academic components of school. Be that as it may, I was still determined to make the best out of one last musical pilgrimage to Hershey, PA.

I arrived at the Hershey Lodge in late March for another week filled with hours of rehearsal, wisdom from a guest conductor, and as a special treat from the Lodge, a seemingly endless supply of Hershey's chocolate milk during breakfast. If there's one weakness to my constitution, it's a sweet tooth. But, what the hell, there are worse vices.

I settled in after my arrival and began the reaudition process to determine seat placement. Every PMEA festival requires a reaudition where students either confirm or change their ranking in the ensemble. All-State Band is unique from district and regional events because there are no preliminary seat assignments. Unlike district and regional auditions, which are influential in determining student progression from one festival to another, most All-State reauditions only concern seat placement in the ensemble and thus lack the drama and intensity of those before them.

The final reaudition of my PMEA career was relatively nonchalant. I was rather pleased with my performance, but I entered the stage for reseating without any significant expectations.

"Alright, first clarinets," dictates the host director from the conductor's podium. He squints, adjusting his glasses while looking down at a clipboard.

"Ok, first I have..."

Last names begin rolling off the list, all unfamiliar to my attentive ear. The first seat is taken, then the second, the third, someone finds the fourth, now we're already at the fifth. He continues listing foreign names.

Damn, I think to myself, *did I really bomb the reaudition that badly?*

"Now Simons, then Brock." He stops after mine, implying that it is I who will occupy the very last seat in the first clarinet section.

My jaw drops in disbelief. I plop myself down in the last chair and sulk.

So much for a good view.

"Ah, wait! Hold on here clarinets." He squints even closer at the clipboard, scanning it up, down, and sideways.

"Sorry everyone, I made a huuuge mistake." His face flushes as he clears his throat and looks up at us.

"I flipped the names by accident. Everyone trade seats from last to first."

"Brock," he notes, "you're first chair."

We all look at each other, exchanging expressions of horror or redemption, and begin collecting our things.

I pick my jaw up off the floor with my instrument. A few steps to the right usher me past the other clarinets to my newly assumed position at the end of the stage. I organize my music and gaze out to the right. There's nothing but empty seats and a cool breeze from the auditorium draft.

First chair. In the All-State Band. The best possible position for a clarinetist in this state-wide ensemble. At my last festival.

Could this new section leader really be the same young clarinetist from all those years ago, the same kid who was determined to avoid failure in his search for success, bombed four lines of sight-reading, regrouped with his lesson teacher, prepared for the next audition with a fire under his ass, and then found himself earning a spot in the All-State Band for two consecutive seasons?

I never imagined such a comeback from number twenty-five to a spot at the top, but here I am, absorbing the sensation of this first chair as other sections are reseated. It feels as if I'm the protagonist in someone else's fiction, ready to climb a mountain with no certainty as to how great the view is from its peak. Or perhaps there's really no such thing as fiction—just stories meant to test our imagination and beliefs regarding all those "real" things in this abstract universe.

The world works in mysterious ways. In any case, my reality sets in: I'm the first chair.

I turn left as my stand partner, the one called "Simons," sits down beside me. He's of medium build with styled brown hair and rimmed glasses, beaming with a positivity unmatched by any previous stand partner of mine.

"Hey, I'm Luke," he says. "Great to meet you, and congrats on first chair!"

"Nice to meet you Luke, I'm Adam. And thank you, I really can't believe it. Congrats on second chair."

He puts down his clarinet as it's apparent we'll be waiting for a while.

"I'm looking forward to working together, can't believe it's my last festival."

"Ah, so you're a senior too? Where from?"

"Just outside the Allentown area, you?"

"Outside of Philly, just shy of the city limits."

"Good stuff man. Hey look," he points, "I think that's our conductor!"

I follow the line of his finger to see a distant figure enter the back of the auditorium. He ascends the podium after reseating is completed.

"Hello everyone, my name is Shannon Kitelinger and I'll be your host conductor for this year's All-State Band. I'm a professor at San Diego State University, and like many of you, come from Pennsylvania. We have a great program lined up and I'm looking forward to working with everyone."

Kitelinger spares little time getting into rehearsal. He leans over to me during our first break to discuss one of the highlights in our program, David Maslanka's *Requiem*.

"Hey, wanted to let you know that there's a big clarinet solo towards the end of *Requiem*. We'll be working on it later today."

I clear my throat before responding, hoping my wide-eyed anxiety doesn't sneak through a facade of confidence.

"Ok, ah that's, great. Can't wait to play it."

He leaves the stage and I fervently dig through my folder for the Maslanka solo. There it lies, tucked away at the top of the last page. The tempo marking indicates a slow forty beats per minute with nothing but ostinato piano accompaniment and the natural pulse of Kitelinger's baton.

Just piano accompaniment at the start. In other words, I'll be practically alone.

I practiced my music before the festival, but never thought that any part marked "solo" would be of any relevance.

Luke turns to me before leaving the stage.

"A solo!" he exclaims. "That's great news!"

I murmur softly to avoid cracking my voice. Like my miraculous ascension to the first chair was going to come with no strings attached.

"Yeah," I mumble, "gonna be a fun one."

***

While there was no rain-inspired improvisation at this year's All-State Band, I was gifted with a different surprise altogether.

Luke and I get up from the stage on what is now our third day of rehearsal. We hear the call for lunch break and rush to quickly clean our instruments. If music is the first priority at PMEA festivals, then the second is undoubtedly food.

"Hey Luke," I ask, "did you happen to be at All-States last year? You looked familiar."

He takes a sip of water. "I was on first clarinet last year, first chair second row. You?"

"Oh yeah," I reply, "third chair in the second clarinets. You had a nice flow going last year if I recall correctly?"

I don't normally notice stuff like hair, but some things are hard to forget.

"Yes," he smiles, fighting through a laugh. "My flow and I were in last year's band together."

I grab a tray as we move through the lunch line.

"Crazy that we've been here for two years now. You got any plans for after high school?"

"I'm going to pursue clarinet," he declares. "Looking at Rutgers or Temple for clarinet performance, maybe musical theater as well. You?"

His conviction is impressive. The guy knows what he wants.

"I'm going to Temple," I reply. "Like the school and the surrounding opportunities in Philly. Hope to see the Philadelphia Orchestra, sports teams, whatever else comes up."

"You're a sports fan?" He turns his head with a bright look in his eyes. "Me too man, I love baseball, played it all my life."

A baseball player? I think. *Finally, another serious clarinetist who enjoys sports!*

"No shit that's great," I respond, "am a hockey player myself. Gotta be my favorite activity other than music."

"Can imagine so, the Flyers are a great franchise."

Luke finishes grabbing his food and we sit down at an empty cafeteria table.

"I'm also really drawn to the sports scene around Philly. Who knows," he says, "if I study at Temple, then maybe we'll play together in another ensemble one day. Catch a game too!"

I look up between bites of my sandwich, struggling to contain a smile.

"Stranger things have happened."

It might have taken me till my last festival, but I finally found much more than just a stand partner in my new friendship with Luke Simons. I was once told before my first PMEA festival that some of the people I'd meet at these events would become friends for life. This statement could have been no truer.

Luke Simons is a man who lives by his passion. He abides by his own creed of music and sport, an extremely refreshing combination for someone like me. Though I have no idea how his reaudition went, I am confident we were brought together by a force greater than PMEA judging.

I view my friendships with Luke Simons and Chris Rinaldi in the same light. Both individuals hold parallel positions in my life and are just that: individuals driven by passion for the activities they love. Chris and Luke were all I needed to prove some of the sincerest friendships begin in unexpected moments. These two friends are also another compelling justification for pursuing passion. The opportunity to meet your next best friend, future business partner, or significant other might just be waiting for a leap of faith on the things you love.

Too bad PMEA experiences aren't solely about starting new friendships. While I find great convenience in musing over ideas other than my musical abilities, the performance of my Maslanka solo creeps closer by the second.

I shudder at the thought of playing quietly for my fellow musicians, hundreds of passionate families, and more than enough recording equipment. I am thrilled for this chance, a once-in-a-lifetime opportunity to lead my section in the All-State Band. What I never planned for was soloing in front of an audience from all around the Keystone State.

There's no hiding in this business, let alone as the first chair. My solo is a naked one and will be far more exposed than any musical contribution I've made thus far as a PMEA participant. From my earliest moments with cassette tapes to the 2016 All-State Band, the penultimate event of this festival, and perhaps my entire musical journey, is drawing near.

I just hope I'm ready.

REQUIEM

Concert day arrives after half a week in the first chair. I stroll to my seat around 10:15 a.m. on April 2nd, 2016 with Luke Simons at my side. He wears the bright white and gold-trimmed marching band uniform from his high school, a PMEA tradition, while I am dressed in a traditional black tuxedo.

This performance is about more than just a solo. As I look out from my seat at an audience gathered from all over the Keystone State, I wonder about my future as a musician. My PMEA journey has almost come to an end and I teeter on the edge of a seesaw between my passions for music and hockey.

I am a sentimentalist, and although I satisfied my appetite for each activity over the past few years, part of me worries that this could be the end of my time as a performer and athlete. The upcoming performance could change my heart and convince me to pursue the path of a professional musician or collegiate ice hockey player. Then again, I might leave this final concert with greater resolve to balance my passions in the future.

Who will I be after today's show? An athlete, musician, or something in between?

All thoughts of the future aside, there is one fact that remains undeniably certain: I am the first chair clarinetist in the 2016 PMEA All-State Band for at least another hour and we have work to do.

Kitelinger's pre-concert speech maintained the same intensity as Balmages' but was of a rather different flavor. One of his most moving points came from Maslanka's *Program Note* for *Requiem*, the piece whose long clarinet solo I will soon display. After reflecting on the tragedy of World War II, Maslanka composed *Requiem* to honor the unknown victims of past conflicts. He also wrote this piece for individuals experiencing changes in their lives. (Program Note, Requiem, 2021)

The All-State Band prepares for Maslanka's reflections on the past approximately seventy-one years after the end of World War II. As if the act of performing any solo isn't complicated enough, I now sit here praying that my upcoming contribution will be sufficient to meet Maslanka's powerful intentions.

Requiem is second in the concert program and I take several deep breaths after applause dies down from the opening piece. Kitelinger then lifts his baton, makes eye contact with the clarinet section, and begins our performance of *Requiem*.

A slow, repetitive pulse emerges from the clarinets and becomes the heartbeat of the band. Accompaniment comes and goes, uniting the clarinets with the piccolo, saxophones, percussive flares, and an ever-present triplet piano ostinato in the background. Hollow sounds creep over the stage and cover the audience like fog over an English moor.

The band then travels onward in a different key altogether, gaining speed and traction by the second. We gradually climb the chromatic scale, changing pitches in the smallest incremental steps possible as we claw our way to the top of a chord whose name I can't imagine. This roller coaster called *Requiem* then crests the top of its tracks and plunges downward into all the suffering endured during the early 1940's. I let go of my seat belt and brace for the ride ahead with fingers flying all over my clarinet.

We cycle through a damned ritual, resurfacing for air after deep, spiraling symphonic dives. The whole group descends in unison: clarinets, flutes, baritone sax, even an assortment of xylophones and marimbas. Maslanka's explosive reckoning with World War II bombards the audience before time stalls across the ensemble.

My body prepares for my upcoming solo in this moment of silence between death and rebirth. The back straightens and arches, both feet rest firmly on the floor. My upper body conforms to the first chair and both eyes fixate themselves on my part and the temporary stillness of Kitelinger's baton.

My heart rate slows by the second as I wait for our return to metrical time. The blood rushing through my veins gradually decelerates in anticipation for that slow, ostinato marking of forty beats per minute. My body is ready in all but one crucial component: my nerves.

I drilled the deceptively simple rhythms and pitch changes into my fingers and mental soundtrack for days, using every opportunity from run-throughs of *Requiem* to lunch breaks with Luke and other clarinetists. Musicians say to "practice like you perform," for doing anything else is a distraction from the ideal product. This strategy may address the technical elements of a performance, but it did not quell my fear of making a mistake with the All-State Band.

I really only have one shot, a single chance to evoke the necessary emotions from our audience. Live concerts are in fact interactive, even if listeners may not recognize it. There is always a give and take between performers and audience, a cyclical push and pull of presentation and response that makes live music such a unique experience.

Performances with mistakes are undoubtedly still performances, but serious musicians understand that each and every error in a "classical" setting brings them further from the composer's original intention. Variations are desirable in some genres like free-form jazz, but my goal to provide the audience with an authentic version of *Requiem* leaves no room for error.

There is no reaudition, no second try, no thought of redemption. I have one opportunity to get this right.

The piano dissolves our silence with a heavy, repetitive triplet figure. I sit still, watching the measures go by as that solo has finally arrived on my doorstep, begging to be performed. The triplets crescendo ever so slightly as Kitelinger leads the group towards my entrance.

He turns, glancing over to check that I'm ready. I can see Luke grinning slightly out of the corner of my eye as each beat drags me closer to my solo. I readjust my posture, fully open my airway, and remove any miscellaneous spit from my reed. Thoughts of World War II, Maslanka's note, the reaudition, last year's All-State festival with Balmages, and even my first failed audition flood my mind as I focus on the first three notes. My heart decelerates to match the piano at forty beats per minute.

It's just two eighth notes before a sustained open G.
Easy done.

I steady myself for the impending tightrope walk with no net to catch my fall, no one to hold my hand as musical time shoves me up against a wall.

Six beats to go, now four.
Get ready!

The gigantic rectangular concert room is full of eyes, so many eyes, all locked in on the young, first chair clarinetist as he leans forward to play. I gently move air upwards out of my lungs. It strikes the corners of my mouth and eventually exits through my embouchure. The air spins and spirals, bouncing inside my cylindrical wooden clarinet as those first three notes propel my solo into the spotlight.

I match Kitelinger's slight changes in tempo, pulling, lagging, and steadying musical time as he offers a path forward. Each and every note gracefully paints itself onto Maslanka's musical canvas; I offer my condolences to those lost in conflict, all the souls who cried out in their final moments and likely heard nothing in return. My body sways from side to side as those eyes remain fixated on my contribution to *Requiem*.

The fragility of my first sight-reading stands in complete contrast to this solo performance. I steady my fingers with ease and there's not a confusing E# in sight. The first flute eventually joins me and I project my final sustained G with a steady hand, sweeping aside the tension of an Ab to offer peace to all players and listeners. The G trails off to an entrance from other clarinets that moves us towards the end of Maslanka's composition.

Kitelinger guides us musicians, the audience, all recording personnel, and Hershey Lodge staff to a final coming to terms with the Second World War. The piano is the last instrument to finish off a message of unity for the future and gives way to the same magical silence after Balmages' piano improvisation.

We rise to accept the crowd's subsequent applause. I smile and fight off the shakes as the All-State Band stands proudly, cloaked in a tremendous sea of ovation.

I knew not exactly where I was going, or doing for that matter, when I began my journey to the All-State stage over three years ago but left that final PMEA concert in awe of it all. Music facilitated new friendships, brought me somewhere close to the rain with Brian Balmages, and processed world tragedy in Maslanka's *Requiem*. My failures, festivals, relationships, and ultimate pursuit of passion yielded opportunities like this All-State Band solo. Some memories are impossible to forget and these are no exception.

As I walk away from the stage after the concert and wave goodbye to Luke, I'm left to reckon with who I've become. Am I still that young clarinetist caught up in his ego and resistance to anything but success, or perhaps a lofty first chair instrumentalist destined to pursue music and discover some artistic catharsis? Did I conform to the norms for musicians and athletes, or actually carve myself a path between sport and art that's shared by others like Luke Simons?

I'd argue it's something of a mix. My reflection in the mirror still shows that same old Adam Brock, the kid who sang in the car with his family and advertised his hockey team as a sixth grader. I've no doubt collected new experiences from PMEA, both the hard lessons gained from failure and the immense satisfaction from investing in my passions.

Things all around me have certainly changed; the world isn't what it used to be back in 2013. These last few years have indeed been a balancing act between sufficing my interests in the arts and athletics while following the academic path of any high school student. Though I leave this final concert without some final push to go all-in on music performance, I can sleep well knowing that I left it all out on the stage as a PMEA participant.

There is but one thing left undetermined after all these adventures from the last few years, a piece of my high school puzzle still missing from the set.

I haven't unveiled what the hell I'm going to study in college.

There are no dual hockey-music degrees at Temple University, and even if I did find such a program, I'm not so sure what I'd be preparing myself for after school. Then there's the question if my dual passions will survive a full four years of investment in another discipline.

It never hurts to be selective when making these big choices, and as I approach the final months of high school in the aftermath of this All-States event, fate would have it that help for my degree choice was on the way. I'm enrolling at Temple University, that much is certain. My anticipated major, rather than solely focusing on music or sports, is a subject that meets them halfway.

ARMS WIDE OPEN

"Brock, I simply cannot do the generic HAGS. This deserves something better."

Eric Scheidly looks down at my high school yearbook with frustration. We sit in the front his physics classroom, surrounded by equations and derivations from classical mechanics to abstract concepts of electricity and magnetism.

Scheidly's presence alone is enough to make a large room feel small. His towering figure and razor-sharp gaze slice through the air with the confidence of a man who made physics and science education his life. He shuffles in his seat, placing one brown, rugged cowboy boot on top of the other as his writing hand steadily holds a thin black pen above the crisp white pages of my book.

"It's all you Scheidly," I reply. "We know these things can't be rushed."

My legs dangle over the side of a sturdy student desk while I bathe in natural sunlight. The four principal Maxwell Equations rest on a set of large windows in faded blue dry erase marker while their integral forms await proper application in all types of problems from Scheidly's AP Physics course. College Board exams have come and gone, and the sun shines on June 1st, 2016 as I, along with the senior class, enjoy the last few days of high school.

His pen suddenly strikes the paper with force, inscribing the product of Scheidly's drawn-out concentration. I wait eagerly in anticipation as he digs into the page and carves out his personal contribution in my iconic high school keepsake. He shifts his hand slightly downward to a new line and finishes his note with a well-practiced signature. Scheidly stares at the writing and looks up, handing me the finished product.

Brock, There is a transition that happens when physics equations stop being math and start being language. *You are one of the rare ones who get that. Eric Scheidly*

I take particular notice of the underline. *Language,* I think, *what an interesting word.* Though one may not normally think of physics, mathematics, or even science itself as language, I absolutely concur with Scheidly. Physicists manipulate algebraic symbols not out of mathematical interest, but rather to describe the balance of power in nature. They analyze physical forces swirling in the mosh pit of the natural world, dragging particles as small as electrons to masses of planetary proportion onto their theoretical lab tables for examination. From linear equations to the integration and derivation of vector and tensor quantities, physics unlocks all those secrets of the universe in a way that man can understand them. Humankind may never know if nature was designed to express itself in a logical, mathematical fashion, but physics nevertheless explains (most of) the phenomena surrounding all things and their existence.

Scheidly returns a nod when I look up to speak, raising his hand as a sign of everything that need not be said. I close my book and maneuver off the desk.

"Thanks Scheidly, see you later."

"No problem Brock!" rings out behind me as I exit the scientific epicenter of Plymouth Whitemarsh High School.

I had only taken one physics class in 2014 before this AP adventure with Scheidly. In Honors Physics, Jim Muscarella taught me that the most basic interpretations of natural law yield a great many observations about everyday macroscopic life like a car decelerating on the road, baseballs flying in parabolic arcs, and collisions between billiard balls. However, it was only through further analysis in Scheidly's legendary AP course that I explored the fundamental behaviors of the universe and turned over the garden rock to examine all the tiny organisms, microscopic environments, and scientific marvels I would have otherwise never investigated.

Scheidly wasted no time in guiding me through these secrets and I never stopped digging. Such was my motivation to finally answer the call of what to pursue at Temple University: a physics degree with the goal of becoming a high school science teacher.

I have always loved education, whether that's in school, on the ice, or during rehearsal. But pursuing *physics*? What about those other passions I already spent so much time exploring? Have I come this far only to turn my back on the past?

Physics, for me, was a language connecting my love of sports, passion for the arts, and interest in education. The subject offered a gateway to both my passions while simultaneously supporting my intended career as a high school teacher. It was not my anticipated college major during the first three years of high school, but Scheidly redefined my interest in the natural world through physics. The next logical step after his AP course was then to complete my university studies as a physics major, though certainly not before the penultimate event of my high school education.

Graduation ceremonies begin just one week after Scheidly inscribed *language* into my yearbook. Wednesday June 8th, 2016 marks the end of my era at Plymouth Whitemarsh High School. I'm dressed in a gown of blue and red and sit alongside my classmates on the football field. We wait in eager anticipation of our final goodbye to life as high school teenagers.

I walk up onto an elevated stage after my name is called, receive my diploma, and look out into the crowd. My family cheers me on from shining metal bleachers to my left while a slight breeze ruffles my attire. I gaze above my peers in the field before me and stand in awe of the pristine sunset. The Class of 2016 celebrates its achievements at that time just before dusk when the buildings, trees, cars, and birds all fade to black silhouettes. A warm, inviting orange glow coats the treetops and gently fades into a dark blue hue up above. The border between both colors marks the gentle transition between new and old, beginning and end.

My position on this stage must be the top of the world. Like the indecisive boundary between sun and horizon, I stand between one life and another. Today marks the end of a twelve-year career in public school, the final ascent of a mountain supported by over a decade's worth of memories.

I eventually leave the stage and rise from my seat with the rest of my class at the conclusion of all ceremonial proceedings. We take our caps in hand, wait for the signal, and then launch them into the air. They rise higher and higher, sneaking a glimpse above that retreating sunset and indeed into my future. I stare up, wondering which one will fall my way like the unknown experiences, challenges, and growth which await me at Temple University.

My cap disappears in a sea of colors while I think back to the defining moments during high school. With hockey, music, and physics at my side, I head forward into the unknown with a means to march at my own pace, to navigate both internal and external pressures with the tools of my adolescence. Perhaps the path I find myself on today is already established, part of some conveyor belt into the future. Part of me agrees, arguing I found my own means of conformity in a general sense of nonconformism. On the other hand, I could claim it was through nonconformity that I tiptoed over the preconceptions of being both that "music guy" in the rink or the (seemingly) tough hockey player on stage.

In either case, the undeniable source of my pursuits remained the same: passion. My experimentation with passion was the most critical aspect of these last four years. No decision at the end of high school with regard to where, what, or how I should transition to college would have been easy or convenient without such investment in the things I loved.

I argue all individuals, regardless of age, should investigate their passions. This is even more crucial if your interests diverge from the conveyor belt of life and subvert others' expectations because there may be no more powerful force to take a leap of faith than yourself.

Investment in passion does not necessarily require a professional pursuit of one's interests. Take Luke and Rinaldi as counterexamples: one prepares for the career of a full-time musician while the other pursues hockey while finding his way into the communications field. Despite all differences in our futures, the common denominator between their stories and mine is the exploration of passion. Their navigation of interests and professional goals leaves me wondering about yours:

What are your passions?

Have you honored or hidden from them?

What have you done and what will you do about their influence in your personal life and professional ambitions?

If you turned your back on them once before, are you prepared to do so again?

Are you finally ready to take a new leap of faith on your interests, whatever they may be?

The decision of *how* to use your passion is entirely yours. All I ask is that you make one.

As those graduation caps reach their peak and begin a downward descent, the one question left unanswered is if my current life plan is resilient enough to survive the transition to college. Though studying physics sounds reasonable, I truly have no idea what Temple will offer. Life is seldom a direct route; there will undoubtedly be pit stops, traffic, accidents, and rerouting. The question is not if my trajectory will bend but by how much. Will the curvature be too great for my current ambitions, ripping the glue between my field of study and passions? What unanticipated forces and external pressures will come into play?

Such thoughts offer no easy solutions. The collective journey forward is always fraught with uncertainty and my only option, so it seems, is to embrace the coming change and a new period in my life.

The eventual return of my cap to the football field, wherever it may be, clears my view of the fading sunset. In discussing the works of Jean Paul, Claudio Magris notes in his *Danube* how "travelling is perhaps always a journey toward those distances that glow red and purple in the evening sky...to the countries where the sun is rising when it sets with us."

I stare out at the fading light with plans to travel like never before. Temple University, the life of a physics major, and those "red and purple distances" await me on the other side of the setting sun. Taking one final breath, I say goodbye to today with my arms wide open for the new chapter that is tomorrow.

TEMPLE UNIVERSITY

BREAKDOWN

"Bye guys, see you later, love ya!"

I wave goodbye to my mom and brother after our final embrace. They drop me off at the center of Temple's campus and begin the short walk toward Broad Street, one of Philadelphia's largest roadways. The pair turns a corner and exits my line of sight. I keep staring at Broad, hoping they'll change direction and reappear for one last wave. They don't.

I take time to collect myself with a deep breath and start walking to my new home in Philadelphia. I arrive at my building, enter my room, and begin what seems like a never-ending cycle of unpacking. Today goes by as uneventfully as the next five to follow and my last week of summer is over before I know it, leaving hardly a trace in the muggy heat of late August 2016.

I lie on my bed and stare at the ceiling with less than twenty-four hours before my first class. All the movies, TV shows, and stories about the American college experience are finally being put to the test. After turning out the lights and sinking deep into my mattress, I doze off with the knowledge that my preconceptions about university life are about to face the music.

My phone alarm gently lifts me out of a dreamy slumber. I spring off my bed and waltz over to the closet. The first day of college requires a carefully planned outfit: khaki shorts, a

German soccer jersey, Adidas Sambas. I collect a breakfast of cinnamon granola bars and mango juice after admiring my cleanly shaven face in the bathroom mirror. Then I fetch my backpack, tip-toe out the front door of my building, and eagerly head to my very first physics class.

I stroll through campus under crisp blue skies and puffy white clouds. The opening physics lecture sets the stage for what appears to be a hearty semester full of review from Scheidly's class and exploration into several new topics. I fill my breaks between classes with a collection of classical, jazz, and rock music from my orange iPod Nano, and dissolve into a sea of students after my final lecture for the day. My fellow classmates waste no time organizing pick-up Frisbee games, ordering from food trucks, and sunbathing on grassy areas within the so-called "Beury Beach" while I stop by a water ice stand. Hints of frozen mango and strawberry blend with thoughts of Newton's Laws as I head back to my room.

I return with hardly any homework and proceed to shower in what seems like a never-ending supply of hot water. Then I prepare for bed early, turn out the lights, and nestle under my covers.

It takes several reminders from a snoozed phone alarm to pull myself out of a hazy daze. My eyes crack open, skin oily and slick to the touch. I fight through grogginess and stagger into the bathroom. A flick of the light switch reveals a grungy five o'clock shadow, exactly what should be expected after a week of neglect. My back-up phone alarm sounds again at 7:45 a.m. and I dash back into my room and throw on whatever gets me dressed the quickest for an 8:00 a.m. lecture. I rush out the front door in search of my first class and stumble into a seat at 8:01 a.m., only half awake.

My stomach begins to grumble by late afternoon. I arrive at a dining hall before closing time but sit alone. My physics homework is extensive and made even less enjoyable with the lack of workspace in my room. There's been no time for music today, though I did manage to catch some preseason coverage of the Philadelphia Flyers. Tonight's shower lacked any significant water pressure but was just warm enough to soothe the bags under my eyes. I lug myself back up onto my saggy mattress and pray for a full-night's sleep.

Jackhammers sound a premature alarm at 4:00 a.m. I toss and turn in sweaty sheets before dozing off, desperate for rest in the third week of school. My eyes pop open to a frightening realization.

Damn, I curse under my breath, *class begins in a few minutes!*

I tumble out of bed, not even bothering to greet the mirror, and throw on whatever's sprawled out on the dusty floor in front of my dresser. Forget about breakfast, there's no time. My first step out the front door lands in a fat, murky puddle that splashes up onto my pants. Damp patterns formed by the water mirror my scruffy facial hair. Who knows when actually I made it to the lecture.

Cloud cover accompanies my lonely trip to the dining hall for dinner. I drag myself into the food court and sit alone once again. I quickly walk back to my room through a light drizzle while the cup of lukewarm tea in my hand grows colder by the second. I skip showering and crawl into the fetal position on my bed without a shred of energy for homework. Today's physics lecture was rather tough and deviated greatly from the topics I already learned in depth with Scheidly. My iPod sat patiently on my charger all day, simply forgotten during the morning rush.

There's no hockey to watch tonight and my clarinet sits untouched on the northern side of campus, crammed inside a tiny music locker. I lean up after laying down and clamp both hands over my ears, eager to mute the collection of irregularly paced sounds coming from down the hall. Maybe I'll sleep a few hours. Probably less than them, who knows.

So, this is college. I am a tea kettle ready to toot and whistle at any moment from the frustration boiling inside me. Each new week furthers the same trend, driving me farther into a downward spiral. Physics lacks the gusto of my high school experiences, there's hardly any room for music, and I have no time to even think about hockey. My internal scales feel as if they're shifting much too far in one direction, threatening the very balance I came to achieve at Temple.

There is no shame in failure, but *I* won't be failing within the first month of college. It cannot, should not, must not happen. PMEA taught me that struggles were bound to occur in the next stage of life, but I never fathomed encountering them so soon. There is but one hope for relief after these first few weeks of my university introduction: I'm meeting my parents for lunch at the end of September. If I can survive our inevitable discussion about college, then maybe I can handle myself and grind through my first semester.

I slip away from campus on the day of our meeting with delight. It's time to step back, take a deep breath, and enjoy my parents' company. I take the subway and meet them in front of the Eastern State Penitentiary, a famous old prison in the Fairmount section of Philadelphia. We cross the street to a Greek restaurant called Zorba's Tavern and sit down at a table on the sidewalk. I always wanted to eat at Zorba's and gaze hungrily at the entrees being delivered to the customers around us. The sunny afternoon weather is perfect for outdoor eating, though the forecast calls for clouds in the evening.

Our food arrives quickly and we chat about my day, updates at home, and my brother's high school classes. My parents have always been there for me and there have never been many secrets between us. However, the likely focus of today's meal might be the one thing I've failed to mention in the past few weeks.

"So pal," asks my mom, "anything interesting to report at school?"

I put down both utensils with no interest in the appetizing dish sitting before me. An answer to my mom's question is caught in the back of my throat, helplessly lodged in place. Both eyes begin to water as the unease festering in my stomach spreads throughout my entire body. There's no holding back the impending rupture.

Waterfalls suddenly engulf both cheeks. My throat opens to a whimper and accompanies the tears streaking down my face with an acute sense of embarrassment. The other patrons must surely be taking notice of the festivities, though I doubt this was anywhere on the specials menu.

"I miss home so much!" escapes through my sniffles and sobs. I can't bear to look up.

"High school ended so well and I felt so sure about how things would go in college. Ha, what a joke! Everything is completely different than I imagined. I'm surrounded by frat parties, can't sleep, can't catch a break from my studies, can hardly shower."

I soak the napkin on my lap and slobber on.

"I can't find enough privacy, have practically no community with my peers, and I don't feel in touch with almost any of my classes."

All sounds of eating on the other side of the table give way to my snot and sniffles. The sun disappears behind fast-moving clouds as screeches on the sidewalk suggest some patrons are moving their chairs. I can only guess which direction...

"The students I met show no interest in leaving their social cliques, especially with someone that doesn't 'fit into the system' like I am right now. They complain about their parents, families, and high school when those are the things I miss the most."

My parents sit silently while I keep my face down on the table, unable to meet their gaze.

"Why was I so eager to move out at the end of high school? All I do is miss my former life, and it seems I'm the only one that isn't overly thrilled by this new college adventure. I thought I set myself on the right path, but honestly, all I really want is to go home."

I finally lift my head off the table and put both hands over my face. I can't even blend in on the sidewalk at Zorba's, let alone assimilate with university life. Then there's the incoming storm clouds, the baklava topping off this Greek meal of ours. Subtle winds rattle the table as we sit there silently, collecting shards from the shattered picture that was my expectation of college.

I once learned from my favorite video game *R.U.S.E.* that Eisenhower called plans "useless", but planning "indispensable." My first few weeks at school were enough to confirm the first half of this quote, and while I enrolled at Temple with specific plans for the future, my breakdown proved that almost no strategy survives first contact with the obstacles it is meant to overcome. The unpredictability of this new college experience and all those things I did not foresee as a naive teenager had finally jostled my trajectory.

I grew even further detached from my plans from the end of high school after meeting my parents at Zorba's. My major challenge then became not to change my feelings towards this situation, but rather understand my current path was not providing the balance I sought between my passions and career aspirations.

Though my plans were certainly disturbed by a rocky start to freshman year, there was some room for flexibility. I still had control over my major, involvement on campus, and attitude towards this new situation. There had to be some way I could adapt and prove the second half of Eisenhower's quote. I needed a new perspective, different options, something unexpected to stir the pot of my first semester. As the next few weeks began to take shape, I had no doubt that change was on the horizon.

DISSENT IN AMERICA

Sunlight sneaks through the open window in my room and spills over me and my bed. It illuminates dust particles reminiscent of past years, critical decisions, and histories defined by perpetual change.

I sit hunched over my computer, bouncing back and forth between an abundance of Chrome tabs. They all share one similarity: Temple's class registration software. I scroll through endless lists of electives, caught up in a caffeine-inspired rush and the thrill of the chase. Today's exploration of almost every undergraduate offering in Fall 2016 has yielded some fascinating results: entire courses devoted to Shakespeare, the chemical analysis of wine, glassblowing. I suppose they have to find enough things for more than twenty-five thousand undergraduates to study.

I suddenly break my cycle of repetitive searching and click on one particular class description.

It reads "Dissent in America."

Dissent, I wonder, *what does that mean again?*

My eyes scan the course details, schedule, and availability. One particular statistic catches my attention: there's already ninety-nine seats filled in a section capped at one hundred students.

One lonely seat left.

I rub my chin after rereading the class description.

Ah, what the hell, let's try it.

I select the "Register Now" button and cross my fingers. My course calendar updates after the page refreshes and confirms my selection of that final spot. A quick rumble from my stomach serves as a reminder for lunchtime and I close my computer, finished with my only schedule change during Fall 2016.

This registration was nothing less than my first true turning point at Temple. Chris Rinaldi already demonstrated the effects of one single decision in middle school, a seemingly insignificant choice that yielded immense and unpredictable changes. Registering for a general education elective was not my last turning point in college, but arguably one of the most consequential.

I would soon learn how America was born out of dissent, forged in the fires of individual decisions to deviate from the norm and work for a better life.

The first step in changing my trajectory came from a similar action. It all began with dissent.

***

I place my laptop into a Temple-themed backpack and head out the front door of my building in September 2016. I arrive at Gladfelter Hall and climb a short flight of steps into my first *Dissent in America* class of the semester. The lecture hall's digital clock displays 1:00 p.m. when I sit down, pull up the desk attachment on my seat, and take note of what must be my new professor.

He walks into the room without hurry. He closes the door gently behind him, strolls to the presenter's desk in a pair of matching black boots, and places a brown leather briefcase down on the small table beside him. Our instructor takes off thin black sunglasses and pauses, slicking back puffs of light gray hair. He loads materials from a flash drive onto the computer and steps back to address his audience.

"Ok, let's get started. Hello everyone, my name is Dr. Ralph Young and this is Dissent in America. Today we'll clarify any questions about the course syllabus and begin discussing acts of dissent in Europe that set the stage for the founding of our nation."

Ralph looks around the room and then begins his lecture. I open my notebook, ready a mechanical pencil, and get to work. Although I had never planned to take any history courses in college, my first few minutes in Ralph's class were a sign I was soon to embark on a journey like no other. Our first few lectures blended easily into the second, third, and fourth weeks of the semester. I was hooked by October, addicted to a drug called dissent.

The weeks pass by with palpable momentum. Ralph Young guides me through the early schisms in the Catholic Church to the birth of Protestantism, the legacy of the English Tudors, and then into an in-depth discussion of dissent on American soil. He brings our class from the settlements at Jamestown to the modern day, collecting pieces of the great American experiment before molding them together to discover how our nation, one which boasts of presidents, wars, and great legislation, was truly shaped by dissidents and protesters. We explore the colonial period up through the Revolution, from the Antebellum to the Civil Rights movement, adding names like Roger Williams, John Peter Zenger, Henry David Thoreau, and Carl Schurz to the large family tree of American dissenters.

I arrive early to every lecture and secure my preferred seat in the third row. My notebook is filled to the brim after each class with names, dates, and dissenters up and down every page. This ordinary binder becomes something more reminiscent of a personal journal, a catalog of America's past through the lens of protest. Our student community follows Ralph through a history less traveled, discovering parts of our country hidden from my grade school lessons and high school education. Each day in *Dissent* is a fresh breath of life and my lungs can't get enough of it.

Protest, I think. *This is America.*

Ralph's course consumes my interest and is the one thing dragging me out of bed in the morning. Though I thought nothing of it at the time, my nonchalant enrollment in *Dissent* actually occurred weeks before my breakdown. I needed another general education elective and Ralph's course turned out to be the change I was looking for after that lunch at Zorba's.

The months of September and October slowly gave way to the coolness of late fall as I continued studying dissent with Ralph. Those autumn leaves may have been gone by the first week of November, but I marched forward into the second half of the semester with dissent as the wind in my sails.

Ralph stands front and center on a day like any other.

"I hope you're enjoying our recent analysis of dissent during the World Wars. Today we begin the Civil Rights movement and approach the start of our research project."

He paces across the room with his black leather jacket on full display.

"You will write a five to seven page research paper on an American dissenter or dissent movement. When picking your topic, you can, of course, choose one of the individuals we've mentioned and studied deeply in class. But then again, studying a movement we haven't analyzed in depth will offer new insight into your understanding of American dissent."

One student raises her hand. "Dr. Young, do you have any guiding questions or themes that we might want to explore?"

"Well," he replies, "there are specific guidelines on the official document which I'll soon post online. However, I would advise you to keep the following questions in mind for all dissent movements."

He clears his throat before continuing.

"What is the nature of their dissent? What is the difference between legitimate grievances and injustices and perceived grievances and injustices? Was their dissent violent, and if so, was it justified? Is violence ever justified? Were your dissenters prophets or crackpots? And, perhaps most importantly, what impact did their dissent have in our free society?"

Ralph clasps his hands together and addresses the entire class.

"I urge you to not only consider these questions for your projects, but also in your everyday lives. Philadelphia, America, the whole world is confronted with the status quo and dissenters. What are we to make of it all? Being an informed citizen involves understanding these questions and their impact, the push and pull so commonly found in America throughout our studies."

I made a crucial realization after digesting Ralph's project description: my first month at Temple was defined by confrontation "with the status quo and dissenters." In other words, I wanted to dissent against my own expectations and the attitude of my peers. I was not ready to conform with university life and fulfill my own personal hopes to love every aspect of college. The stereotypical mold for freshmen was there for the taking and I just didn't fit.

Though I desired change, *Dissent in America* led me to conclude that small deviations may not be sufficient to correct my journey through college. I recognized that dissent, the intentional divergence from my current plans as a physics major, might be the one force powerful enough to redirect my studies and completely resurrect my undergraduate experience.

It became increasingly clear in the last full month of my first semester that I was not the only one considering the role of dissent in society. The United States was at its own turning point, the start of a new age of protest.

***

My phone alarm yanks me out of a groggy daze. Joints crack and pop as I lift myself up and stretch after a sleepless night. My ears perk up from the light, steady rainfall pattering the window and I check my phone for the date.

It's Wednesday November 9th, 2016, and it is a cold day.

A walk outside my building confirms my view from inside. Sheets of rain extract the life out of what would normally be a busy Wednesday morning. Water drips down buildings, snags itself in tree limbs, and withers along the pavement until an eventual greeting with the sewers. I walk up to a telephone pole and find a blue political banner with a woman's face on the front. It's tattered, torn by the winds from last night. Soggy bits and pieces lie at the base.

Even *Dissent in America* is permeated by bleakness. Despite all efforts to the contrary, all fifty minutes of today's lecture are spent discussing the collective confusion, disbelief, and disappointment in America's recent choices.

I spot another blue flyer after class, this one severed into large chunks with a footprint stain in the center. Only the woman's eyes are intact on two torn fragments. The rain's lighter now, and a retreat back to my room is all I can muster. My limbs have given up, devoid of energy as the hours tick by at a snail's pace.

Water droplets are busy aggravating my window when I hear a frantic knock on the door. I get up off my bed and am greeted by a friend from down the hall.

"Do you know what's going on outside? We need to check it out!"

He stares at me with urgency, even anger. I grab my raincoat with haste and follow him outside. He twists his fingers fervently as we enter the subway and travel downtown. We exit the city hall station to the sight of empty streets. No cars, no people. Nothing but the rain. Periodic sirens wail far off in the distance while water spits on our jackets.

"C'mon," he says, "they must've gone north. Let's head back up Broad."

We start running back towards campus, increasing our pace as the rain joins us for a ride. We avoid puddles and debris in a two-mile pursuit of those mystery sounds.

"Look!" he exclaims. "You can finally see it!"

Out of the misty fog appears the biggest mobile police blockade I've ever seen. Cars move together in unison with sirens muffled by some clamor on the other side. Yellow streetlights tint the incessant downpour as we dodge vehicles and the occasional flying puddle. Wet light illuminates our path as my friend and I finally work our way around the barricade.

The lead car follows behind a flurry of activity. Hundreds of Americans dominate the central causeway through North Philadelphia, some carrying banners while others boast cardboard signs. A majority leads the group in chants, speeches, and songs. A city within a city occupies Broad Street tonight; to where they march I know not.

I stay close to my friend while joining the outskirts of the crowd in its slow crawl to Temple's campus. The rain taunts the protesters to continue marching, demanding they trudge forward into the unknown. Members on the fringes of the group call out to private apartments as the dissenters cross Cecil B. Moore Avenue and engage with a restless audience that sends many of its own to join the crowd. I'm absorbed into the mass when people rush in from every direction and block all possible escape routes.

Protesters of all ages and colors constitute the movement, united by collective shock and anguish on this dreary Wednesday in November. They cry out in animated pain and suffering, lamenting the soul of a nation cast into turmoil as beliefs of hope were suddenly trodden underfoot by the announcement of a new and divisive administration. The country is preparing for change, and these Americans want no part of the new government that begins next January.

I think back to Ralph with every step forward. This is American dissent in the flesh, not from our course books, old videos, or impassioned speeches, but real, raw action. A helicopter appears overhead and watches the crowd as we move through campus and continue north. We grow exponentially in size, spilling out onto the sidewalks and further slowing the pace of the police cars behind us.

"There are similar ones happening all across the nation tonight!" shouts one marcher. "The whole country's up in arms. This is only the start!"

I begin to question certain elements of our march as we journey further beyond the northern limits of campus. To my left lies a car, its roof smashed by some blunt object. Battered street signs litter the sidewalk to my right. Protesters topple a van and transform it into a makeshift stage for orators condoning vandalism, only the start of what's apparently to come. My friend and I maneuver out of the crowd as the protest continues heading north, uncomfortable with thoughts of seeing this through to the end. The protest turns left after our getaway and continues shamelessly into the darkness.

Ralph's guiding questions are all I can think about while we wander back to our building. For the first time in my life, I witnessed and partook in a real act of dissent. This protest in Philadelphia was no singularity, for Americans all over the nation took to the streets as we marched up Broad on a Wednesday night in November. It became clear in the following years, if not immediately at the conclusion of tonight's protest, that this was not to be an isolated occurrence.

How one should assess and judge this event is a subject I leave untouched for the moment. My own analysis of the America I know will come in due time. Regardless of interpretation, one must admit the undeniable fact.

A new age of protest was born on Wednesday November 9th, 2016.

This act of dissent was an incredible supplement to my first few months in *Dissent in America*. Ralph's words and assignments were compelling in their own right, and the opportunity to witness American protest on the streets of Philadelphia was more than enough to secure my separation from the physics program.

As my coursework with Ralph eventually came to an end in December 2016, I wondered if dissent's role in my own journey might diminish. My time with Ralph Young had seemingly come and gone, lost to the past like any other college course. I could feel myself leaning towards a different major, career path, or even new life goals altogether at the beginning of my second term, but I was still unsure if protest would play a role in any future decisions.

The year 2017 irrevocably changed my undergraduate experience at Temple, and my second semester finally offered an attractive opportunity to build community on campus. After Fall 2016 primarily focused on dissent, Spring 2017 united the studies of my first term with one of my earliest passions: music.

ELEGY FOR A YOUNG AMERICAN

President John Fitzgerald Kennedy was assassinated on Friday November 22nd, 1963. He was shot while riding in his presidential motorcade through downtown Dallas, Texas. Kennedy died shortly after visiting a nearby hospital.

Five years later, Martin Luther King Jr. was gunned down on April 4th, 1968 at a motel in Memphis, Tennessee. Like Kennedy, King passed after the shooting.

Robert Francis Kennedy was shot two months later in a Los Angeles hotel. He fought for over a day before being pronounced dead on June 6th, 1968.

All three murders erased some of the most promising American political leaders in the 1960s. These savage acts of dissent left a wounded nation, an America horrified and hardly able to process the bloodshed. Various artists, musicians, and film directors crafted their own responses to the JFK assassination over the last sixty years. My favorite reaction to the events of November 1963 comes from American composer Ronald Lo Presti.

The Merriam-Webster dictionary defines an elegy as "a song or poem expressing sorrow or lamentation especially for one who is dead." In his 1964 concert band composition entitled *Elegy for a Young American*, Lo Presti explores the pain and grieving processes brought on by the assassination of America's 35th president. (Theodore Presser Company, 2021) Though he only wrote to the events of 1963, I believe Lo Presti's piece captures similar emotions and agony from the MLK and RFK assassinations in 1968.

All three episodes of violent dissent are on my mind as I sit patiently with my clarinet in the Temple Performing Arts Center. While I always expected to encounter some sort of protest or connection to *Dissent in America* in 2017, I never thought it'd be through concert band.

I spent a great deal of time discussing protest music with Ralph and continued listening to dissenters like Pete Seeger, the singer of *Little Boxes* from the Author's Note, beyond the end of last year. Now, after turning the page to my second calendar year of college, I finally found musical bliss in Spring 2017. I pulled my instrument out of that dusty little music locker and gained admission into Temple University's Symphonic Band, an ensemble primarily composed of music majors under the baton of Dr. Matthew Brunner. Playing with such skilled performers (including Luke Simons and other PMEA friends in a future semester!) revived my passion for music, and I wait on stage in eager anticipation of our performance of *Elegy for a Young American*. For a quality rendition on YouTube, I recommend the 2013 live recording entitled "LO PRESTI Elegy for a Young American – 'The President's Own' U.S. Marine Band."

A silence overtakes the Temple Performing Arts Center as musicians make their final seat adjustments for Lo Presti's *Elegy*. I look up from my chair to observe the magnificent stained glass window above the top row of audience seats. Bits of sunlight sneak through its yellow panes and expose themselves onstage, highlighting a variety of bright brass instruments and melancholy woodwinds. This glow resembles the wet light of last year's protest and that reflective characteristic called dissent. I can see my family waiting eagerly for our performance under the stained glass as a few more performers arrive on stage. We are all dressed in concert blacks; the men wear tuxes, each with slightly different bow ties, while the women shine in elegant dresses. Brunner ascends the podium and accepts applause from the audience. He lets the room grow quiet and then begins *Elegy* with a swing of his light brown baton.

An all-clarinet introduction stuns the concert hall with hollow, empty chords. We repeat a desolate pattern one, two, then three times, highlighting dissonance between collective breaths. Each repetition grows in intensity as more instrumental groups join the somber call and progress up a whimpering C minor scale. Our sound expands outward and bubbles, first on the stage and then over the audience. Lo Presti's desperate chant restarts once again, carrying almost every woodwind and brass player up that painful scale. The swings of Brunner's baton begin to waver, and time slows as we yearn for a pitiful resolution on the highest pitch. It never comes.

The group inches forward as Brunner holds back even further, warping time and auditory space as we shutter in a lack of diatonic clarity. I sneak a glance above my stand before the final pendulum swing of his baton. The percussion section joins the incomplete passage with desperate cries for a safe journey to the piece's conclusion. Yet I know, as Brunner does, that it's never meant to be.

Just one more note. Please don't make us do it.

I've neither seen a man shot nor killed. Hope I never have to. However, on this dreary day in the Temple Performing Arts Center, we're bound to Lo Presti's work by musical law. The

Elegy has a mind of its own and demands that us performers and audience bend to the will of a heartbreaking melody.

Our final act of contempt shocks the concert hall to an agonizing conclusion: we killed JFK.

My sense of time briefly pauses upon arriving to my highest note in that incomplete chord. I can't say how long it lasts, maybe a few seconds at most. What I do know is that my gaze, whether physical or mental, shifts involuntarily upwards to the ceiling. I see an explosion in that moment of melodic pain, a cylindrical beam of light rising up from the ensemble. The innards of the vortex are soft and gentle like the eye of a hurricane. The perimeter of the cylinder is dominated by swirling red light, a painful energy comprised of the collective agony, anger, and suffering endured by Lo Presti and the entire nation after Kennedy's assassination.

The redness cascades upward above the stage, blocks out any light from that stained glass window, and takes precedence over every performer and audience member down below. All those lost souls spill out before us, every last person who must have dropped everything and ran to the television or radio to look and listen in horrific disbelief at the unimaginable headline that President John Fitzgerald Kennedy was assassinated while riding in his presidential motorcade through downtown Dallas.

I listened to Ralph explicitly recount his personal experiences with the JFK, MLK, and RFK assassinations in the few months before this Symphonic Band concert. I was struck by his utter heartbreak at the quick succession of Robert Kennedy after King. He described biking to his apartment at Michigan State University after hearing of Kennedy's murder and screaming out into the darkness, disgusted with the events that had only just recently unfolded, disgusted with a collective deflation now felt after years of civil rights and counterculture protests, and disgusted with the idea that *this is America*, for both the good and certainly the evil which had just recently buried some of the most promising figures of the 1960s.

I continue looking up at the storm with a new sense of perplexing relief, an exhale in this period of borrowed time. Never before had I seen such pent-up emotion in physical form, not even with Balmages' performance and my Maslanka solo at All-States. The vortex reminds me of Jean-Michel Basquiat and his belief that "art" decorates "space" while "music" decorates "time." (Westall, 2021) Just as the artist selects a canvas and creates the right colors, and just as the sculptor chooses the most suitable type of material before chiseling away, so too does the musician arrange and compose in such a fashion to record the past, present, or future in the medium of sound. It's no surprise that music began in ancient times and survived to the modern day, for it has the unique ability to express emotions in time (and sometimes space).

Lo Presti's *Elegy* is one of the few pieces piece that blurs the distinction between art and music, and space and time. As I sit on the stage before Brunner, glimpsing up in the last few moments of that red cylinder, I come to a more funda-mental conclusion: music, like physics, is language. It is the human experience. Scheidly and Maslanka both knew it, and so did Lo Presti when he enshrined the late November of 1963 in this time capsule named *Elegy*.

Despite bombastic scenes with the full weight of heavy brass and scathing woodwinds climbs, Lo Presti does process the events of 1963 with a conclusion of hope for the future. Resolution to an eventual Eb major chord in the quiet finale reminds the performer and audience that we, even in times of incredible crisis, can accept our reality and come to peace with tragedy in our pasts.

One fact was abundantly clear after my performance of *Elegy*: dissent was here to stay. It took me back in time with Ralph, onto the streets of Philadelphia, and now into the concert hall with Ronald Lo Presti. Dissent, like music and physics, is a language. Despite all expectations to the contrary, it transcended the initial disappointments of my freshman year and offered a path to different fields of study besides physics. I smelled dissent on my breath, walked through it on November 9th, 2016, and heard it with the incessant jackhammers.

There was just one problem.

I had no idea where to go with it.

JOHNNY RING

The Johnny Ring Terrace is one of the best-kept secrets at Temple University. Nestled behind the 1940 Residence Hall, this floral hideaway invites visitors down a flight of gray stone steps to find peace and quiet among the hectic routines of main campus. Johnny Ring boasts a wide assortment of gardens, bushes, and birch trees that sway in a slight breeze trickling down from nearby Broad Street.

I descend into Johnny Ring without haste in Spring 2017. The nearby garden features pink, yellow, and light blue flowers as I stretch myself out over a patch of dry grass. Bird chirps mingle with the beeps and honks of bustling traffic, a sobering reminder that this oasis treads above an ocean of cement.

Leaves unfit for autumn cast shadows over my copy of Ralph Young's *Dissent: The History of an American Idea*, one of our two course texts from last fall. I wipe off bits of dust from the cover and find a bookmark resting several hundred pages into this thick chronicle of American dissent. Ralph's work rests firmly in my hands and is a reminder of the individuals and movements that shaped my first college semester and United States history. The blue, grainy hardcover bristles against my palm as I rediscover old friends and foes to the smell of cigarettes being smoked somewhere in the distance.

Pages fall delicately under my fingers in another moment of reflection. Ralph's account of American dissent teases my mind in this second semester, a time demanding seemingly impossible decisions. I paired Symphonic Band with a variety of different coursework to test the waters of my dissent over these last few months, to try and ascertain where I am to go from my first semester. My current course plan reveals English, economics, engineering, and history courses meant to probe Temple's all-you-can-eat buffet of possible degrees. I'm not currently enrolled in any physics courses, though I have yet to officially change my major.

Registration paperwork for Fall 2017 lays crammed in my backpack as I sit with Ralph's book and gaze at the flowers. My decision to dissent brought me to an inflection point and laid the foundation to begin my second year of undergrad with clearer direction. The question of *what to study*, however, remains elusive.

The road before me opens like a five-way intersection. Protest filled my tank, fastened my seat belt, and sat me down before a red light. I'm fully equipped to drive forward but dare not move an inch. Cusses and shouts erupt from behind me when the lights turn green simultaneously. I hear screams and complaints from drivers as their cars remain stuck in place. It'd be easy to blame this traffic jam on my professors and peers at Temple, but the peace and quiet in Johnny Ring reminds me of a sobering fact: the only driver blocking the road is me.

I am responsible for those five lanes forward. Dissent, physics, music, this, that; these choices boggle around in my head like the beads in a baby's rattle. Registration deadlines draw near, my internal pressure bubbles, and I stare aimlessly into the birch trees with almost no idea what to do.

To take a blind leap of faith on the future is to take nothing at all. We must certainly accept certain risks when pushing ourselves closer to the places we want to go, but how do I find the path forward when all five lanes prove no more promising than the others, when I myself am not clear what my current ambition actually is? The pages in Ralph's book provide no immediate solution to my troubles, but there is one long-shot memory that may calm my anxieties.

Ralph concludes a *Dissent in America* lecture at the end of the fall semester by presenting some intriguing flyers. I grab one at the front of the room and pause before sitting back down in my seat, unable to break free of the document's captivating title. It reads "Building Bridges in Derry, Northern Ireland" and describes studying a foreign people, embarking on natural hikes and cultural explorations, and continuing my investigation of history...in Europe. (Temple University, 2018)

I approach Ralph with the flyer held gingerly in hand. He looks up from his computer and spots the pamphlet.

"Hey Adam, have you considered Building Bridges for the upcoming summer? It'd be a great way to continue our work from this semester."

I shrug and nod my head. "It seems really fascinating. You've done this trip before?"

"We ran it two summers ago in 2015. Was an enjoyable experience and we're looking forward to another program."

"We?"

"Yes," he replies. "I run the program with two friends, one from Derry and the other from Germany. Here, take a look."

Ralph gestures to the flyer and shares stories from former hikes, tours of historical sites from some period called the Troubles, and late-night adventures filled with traditional Irish music. He speaks of the town as an old friend awaiting its second pilgrimage by Temple students and professors alike.

The thought of my first European summer was suddenly quite possible. But to study, in Northern Ireland? I never even considered studying abroad during college, let alone in a foreign town called Derry. Of all the different possibilities I encountered in the last few months, this *Building Bridges* trip was surely the wild card.

I return to the present, put down my book, and inhale a deep breath of the tender spring air. In the midst of all my conflicting interests and the different directions laid out before me, it might just be that study abroad, among all the possible choices for the coming summer, is the proper means to clarify my direction at Temple. I'm just not ready to declare a new degree program. A physics major is no longer for me, and the most direct route through that crowded intersection seems to be none other than further studies of dissent. This *Building Bridges* program may not completely address my eventual degree change, but I see only upsides to travel, immersion into a foreign culture, and discussion of Irish protest.

Dissent brought me this far.

I might as well take it to Derry.

A subsequent exhale steadies my thoughts in Johnny Ring. My mental haze settles like residual clouds after an unrelenting storm while bits of sunlight offer temporary resolution to a year's worth of uncertainty. Perhaps for the first time in this second semester, I finally feel a tangible drive for something beyond *Dissent in America* and Symphonic Band.

I'm going to take a leap of faith on *Building Bridges*. My leap will not be blind, but rather the most beneficial route through traffic and the upcoming summer before sophomore year.

The uncertainty of my overall path through Temple still remains frightening, and my dreams of Derry are pixelated. Only Ralph knows exactly what awaits me in Northern Ireland. Despite all apprehensions about the future, I will transform this uncertainty into my biggest ally, the driving force behind discovering my path through young adulthood.

Maybe I'll stick with a science major, switch to something similar like engineering, or even change to a degree in education after this upcoming summer. It could be that this itch called dissent will alter my studies even further, propelling me to a full-time pursuit of my musical endeavors. Regardless of what Derry truly holds in store, I have no shame in shaking up my plans for this first undergraduate summer. Deviating from my original intentions with physics was all but guaranteed by the end of last fall, and the real pity would be doing nothing at all when change knocks on the door of next year's studies. As such, I present my second tool for navigating change: dissent.

Dissent dominated my first year of college like passions dictated my high school experiences. The two also managed to collaborate together, whether that was by connecting my love of music with Lo Presti's *Elegy* or simply contrasting from an otherwise lackluster introduction to Temple. Even more surprising than the influence of dissent was its journey into my life. All it took was a single mouse click, an action without energy, to lure me into a general education course that steadied the turbulence of my first semester.

The influence of dissent in my freshman year was not unique, nor should it be. This decision in Johnny Ring was not my first choice influenced by dissent and I'm convinced it won't be the last.

I believe everyone has a relationship to define with protest against norms, their own plans, and the expectations of others. Let me be clear: analyzing dissent does not always necessitate the subsequent act of dissenting. Just as a leap of faith requires intention and rationale, so too is dissidence only productive with purpose, with some goal or motivation.

The questions we ask ourselves about dissent in society and our own lives prove most useful when preparing for the future we seek. These inquiries may very well demand change, but if not, then they will still offer reflection on the act of protest and its potential to unite your passions and goals. Think back on past decisions:

Did you dissent? Why so?

Did those choices align with your real goals?

Would you make the same decisions again, and if not, are you prepared to dissent if necessary?

I ask myself these same questions to this day. The cycle of endless possibility, choice to dissent or conform, and subsequent analysis will persist for a long time coming. Life offers new challenges every day to conform or dissent from expectations and plans. Regardless of what has already happened, we will always control the *next* opportunity to invest in ourselves and the future.

I packed my bags for Derry after subsequent visits to the Johnny Ring Terrace and the conclusion of freshman year. My departure to Northern Ireland in June 2017 marks one huge step from home; I leave the United States with no regret, ready to take on further studies of dissent with a collection of sleepless nights, protests, and music performances in recent memory. This new journey begins what will hopefully be a long and prosperous summer, one whose adventures and adversity will pave the way to my next step at Temple, whatever that is destined to be.

By trading packed Philadelphia avenues for the cobblestone streets of Derry, I open myself up to the infinite possibilities offered by *Building Bridges*. I can already imagine a shinning glow above the Irish Sea as the storm clouds over my freshman year disappear from view. It is this light that will guide me, illuminating all which awaits in a land whose mysteries far outnumber its certainties on the eastern side of the almighty Atlantic.

DERRY, NORTHERN IRELAND

SLIEVE LEAGUE

Typing begins on a black computer keyboard.

I'm confident I'll receive some great reactions from my family and friends back home from my pictures of rolling hills, flocks of sheep, and views from each mountain top. Yet, despite all my photos, no image can fully capture the feeling of today's hike.

My ears perk up to the chatter of ice cubes in a glass of Baileys at my side. I rock gently in an overused desk chair as the text sinks deep into the fabric of my journal.

It took a collection of connecting flights, caffeinated drinks, and a long wait at immigration, but I finally made it across the Atlantic. Sizzling porridge charmed my nose during a brief layover in London's Heathrow Airport before a rickety propeller plane then introduced me to that shimmering Irish Sea en route to Belfast. From there, I embarked on a three-hour bus ride to Derry, my final destination on the western edge of Northern Ireland. I exited the bus after my arrival in Derry, dropped my bags, and immediately bathed in the late June air.

Moisture from my perspiring fingers drips down the glass of Baileys before I cast it aside and return to my journal. Writing tip number one: avoid drafting after warm showers.

Our walk through Slieve League was one of the most charming natural experiences I ever had. I can't remember a time when I saw more greenery than today on the hike. Over-coming challenging aspects of the trek certainly increased my enjoyment of our journey and made the views even better from atop the highest sea cliffs in Europe.

I am still in awe that a course on American protest facilitated my first European adventure. Choosing to study abroad is one thing, but physically embarking is quite another. The time between departure and arrival was no doubt peculiar; I spent the entire flight bouncing between books, movies, and a pamphlet for *Building Bridges*, edging closer to my destination like a wave at the top of its crest. The subsequent crash and collision with the shoreline were sure to follow, but my body still fidgeted with anticipation, yearning for that first splash forward.

Ralph wasn't kidding.

We were really going to Northern Ireland.

My participation in this month-long study abroad program, like my registration for *Dissent in America*, came from a single decision. I decided to dissent, taking Ralph's suggestion to heart in search of change. Each new experience in Derry is one step closer to fall registration and I accept the task at hand, bowing to all those decisions resting quietly in hibernation before my return home from Northern Ireland.

Today's classroom in early July 2017 was no classroom at all. Our group from Temple left the lecture halls at Ulster University's Magee Campus behind for greener, if not windier, seats along Slieve League in the Republic of Ireland. Located in County Donegal, Slieve League runs along the Atlantic coast, towering above nearby fields and pastures as bright blue waves and buckets of slippery foam flirt with shorelines below. This adventure was the second of six day-long hikes planned around Derry and one the many secrets Ralph concealed in Fall 2016.

I hiked Slieve League with my fellow students and all three *Building Bridges* instructors. Ralph's two co-teachers quickly introduced themselves after my arrival in Derry; Mr. Sean Mullan, a long-time friend from Derry, leads our hiking and cultural programs while Dr. Gudrun Boch of Germany is our expert on Irish literature.

The last drop of Baileys is ample distraction from the fatigue radiating below my waistline, the tribute to those seven hours of ascent, descent, and then further ascent. Our group pressed forward at all elevations while Slieve League proved its designation as the highest sea cliffs in Europe with a peak of nearly two thousand feet above sea level. Rugged hiking boots proudly display stones and debris in the corner of my room and are victims of a sporadic shower from the moist rain jacket hanging on my windowsill.

My hands indent the keyboard like footprints from Slieve League and saturate the sticky keys with memories of mud and sea foam.

I can still feel my boots sinking into the soft Irish ground and the slight give (or large on occasion) in the muddier areas. I could hardly fight back against choppy gusts of wind as we ascended higher and higher, let alone come close to reinventing the smell of Irish sea air.

My exhausted legs can recite campfire tales from that final ascent to what must've been the highest spot on Slieve League, a peak sandwiched between mighty ocean waves and a gentle countryside sprinkled with quaint towns and villages. The ambiance even overpowered my weakest instincts and prompted more than one cringey selfie. To think I still have those photos...

Maybe it's thoughts of my lunch at an abandoned stone house that distract my tongue from the empty glass of Baileys. The ruins were located slightly downhill from an expansive stretch of flat, gray rocks and placated the cries of my wailing, fatigued feet. Our group took refuge beside decrepit, mossy walls and devoured a collection of bagged sandwiches and packed meals. It didn't take long before someone was hit by the right kind of mood.

"Man, wouldn't this be a great time for a blunt!"

There was more than enough agreement to follow.

Our abundance of food stood in great contrast to the poverty of starving peasants who once roamed these stunning green lands. It was only one hundred fifty years ago that the Irish suffered from a horrific famine and scraped by with hardly any means of nourishment. Their suffering prompts my fingers to reengage with the keyboard.

As the saying goes, you can't eat the scenery, and although I might joke over the quip, it really must have been true for all of the courageous folk who left this land of paradise. It must have been a terrible paradox, living in such pristine space with an empty stomach and no food in sight. I always heard of Ireland's green countryside and was probably taught some degree of the island's tumultuous past; yet, despite my background knowledge in Irish history, it seems incredible that conflict and famine occurred in a place of such natural beauty. I imagine there will be much greater reminders and artifacts of the Troubles and general Irish conflict in Derry.

I close my computer lid following the period after *shock*, raise the empty glass, and head outside for an evening walk. Tonight's excursion is no hike along Slieve League; rooftop silhouettes imitate cliffs against the dusky skyline but offer neither greenery nor answers to my questions about this foreign land.

The first step in today's hike was one of many reminders that this summer abroad is no normal college class. I came to Derry, Northern Ireland to study among the Irish, not from thousands of miles away where any foreign study is just that, foreign, incompatible with almost all the senses. Stick out your hand, run the Irish grass through your fingers, taste a Guinness brewed only hours away: this city is real and ripe for investigation.

There is but one message I received from Ralph, Sean, and Gudrun when questioning how to undertake this study abroad program. Such was the theme which dominated the entirety of our trip.

"We will not meander through this experience. Tourism is fine in principle, but actually understanding a foreign people requires thorough and well-rounded investigation of their politics, culture, and history. We must holistically explore every nook and cranny, each and every alleyway to understand the legacy of the Troubles in Derry. Discovering neighborhoods, visiting museums, conversations at the pub; it's simply not enough to casually stroll down main street, take some photos, and move on. The name of this program is our goal during the next four weeks: we are here to build metaphorical bridges between two societies."

They said to explore without hindrance, that every discovery will uncover five new mysteries to unravel. Part of me walks away from such holism, immovably entrenched in doubt that I can really dissect Irish society with an American study abroad program. Another is ready to accept something beyond my inherently American perspective, prepared to improve my world view and embrace a well-rounded investigation of the Northern Irish experience.

These conflicting mentalities prepare for battle with the simplest of questions in mind: *How much will the Emerald Isle change me?*

There remains a third and final part of my being which eagerly mounts the starting blocks before a four-week sprint through Derry. Though my mind tires endlessly from the question of *where* to begin investigating the history of Northern Ireland, there are thankfully other forces at play to facilitate this decision. My second week in Derry presented my first unplanned reminder of the Troubles, an experience which brought me back to last fall at Temple. It went by an all too familiar name: Dissent in Northern Ireland.

TONY TAYLOR

Gravel churns under our bus during another long trip home. I recline in the back row and take a deep, drawn-out breath. Today's hike brought me to the Giant's Causeway, a peculiar collection of hexagonal stone pillars along the Northern Irish shoreline. My nose still tickles from the salty sea air while both legs hang over my seat like those from an oversized rag doll, swaying listlessly after a day-long excursion.

The eventual transition from gravel to asphalt marks a new leg in the journey home. I peek up above the windowsill from my nest of an overflowing backpack and warm rain jacket to catch a glimpse of my surroundings. We're passing through a quaint town reminiscent of Derry; cars boast the same names, flowerpots display the same summer colors, and that distinctive charm of the Emerald Isle permeates every sidewalk, lamppost, and street corner. There is but one pressing difference that catches my eye: this town is smothered in British flags.

Every shop, house, and street sign bear the Union Jack, the iconic flag of the United Kingdom. Its presence evokes memories from a recent lecture on the Troubles, or the period of violent conflict in Irish history from 1968 to 1998 that is the focus of *Building Bridges*. The two primary agitators during the Troubles were the Unionists and Nationalists. Their disagreement stemmed from whether British-controlled

Northern Ireland should remain in union with the rest of the United Kingdom or be nationalized into the Republic of Ireland. Two of the most well-known paramilitary organizations to emerge out of this period were the Irish Republican Army (IRA) and the Ulster Volunteer Force (UVF). (Encyclopaedia Britannica Online Ed, Troubles, 2021)

Derry was a key location during the Troubles. Its position along the border of Northern Ireland and the Republic of Ireland and population of both Unionists, who called the city Londonderry and were predominantly Protestant, and Nationalists, who called the city Derry and were predominantly Catholic, led to a variety of protests and injustices. While opposing forces were often split along religious lines, the Troubles involved discrimination and violent clashes which made the entire period nothing less than a sectarian conflict and struggle for civil rights in Derry and all across Northern Ireland. (Encyclopaedia Britannica Online Ed, Troubles, 2021)

A recent journal entry comes to mind as we leave the Union Jacks behind.

While I learned a great deal about the Civil Rights movement from public high school and Dissent in America, I was never able to combine any knowledge of the past with personal experience at the locations (such as Selma or Birmingham) where significant events took place. However, staying in Derry provides the opportunity to combine knowledge of the Troubles with the locations where they occurred and get a better picture of the whole affair.

I peer away from the window to see Sean rise from his seat and address the few students still awake.

"Make sure to use the upcoming weekend to explore Derry. Check out another unexplored neighborhood, try a new pub, see where the wind takes you. There's so much left to be explored in the city, and with a busier class schedule next week, I advise you take advantage of this time to continue our holistic studies of Irish culture."

My wimpy legs allowed no further exploration after our return that Friday night, but Sean's words were nevertheless on my mind as I rolled out of bed the following morning in early July 2017.

I emerge from my room under watercolor blue-gray skies. I leave my building in Duncreggan Student Village and stroll onto Strand Road, an all-important avenue leading directly to the heart of Derry. My path brings me to the magnanimous Guildhall, one of Derry's famous historical buildings that serves as a meeting place for the city council. It boasts massive stained glass windows, a gigantic pipe organ, and a public courtyard with water fountains and seating areas.

My ears perk up to the sound of a ruckus in the distance and I quicken my pace towards the Guildhall. The commotion I find in today's courtyard paints quite a different picture from its watercolor backdrop. I know this activity like the back of my hand, and it goes by one name only: dissent.

I'm almost eight months beyond my first protest last November, but it doesn't seem like my run-ins with dissidence will be stopping anytime soon. I tip-toe around the fringes of the courtyard and survey the entire scene. Instrumentalists, drummers, speakers, flag bearers, and dancers perform proudly in front of the Guildhall. Protesters at the center of the crowd wear what I imagine to be traditional Irish clothing. They march in place with a multitude of hand-crafted banners and draw in the people of Derry with the following chant.

"FREE TONY TAYLOR! FREE TONY TAYLOR! NO FALSE IMPRISONMENT! LET OUR PEOPLE GO!"

The crowd demands Taylor's release without remorse. Musicians playing drums and long black flutes accompany their shouts with traditional-sounding tunes while demonstrators on the courtyard's perimeter wear T-shirts and hold signs with what must be the headshot of Tony Taylor himself. Police officers stand by as I walk to an older man standing on the fringes of the protest.

"Ah, excuse me," I inquire, "but who is Tony Taylor?"

"Who's Tony Taylor?!" the stranger responds in a fiery Irish accent. "Why, he's the victim of unjust imprisonment! Been locked away with no due cause. He's a man of the Irish people!"

"Arrested for what?"

"Nothing!" shouts the protester. "Used to be an IRA man, was freed years ago after spending some time behind bars, and the police just picked him up again off the street last year. An outrage to say the least!"

He turns back to the crowd and joins in a new chant. I snap a few pictures of the courtyard before selecting the Notepad app on my phone and typing real-time impressions for my journal.

The realities of Bloody Sunday and standoffs in the early 1970s were made even clearer today. Past visits to several museums and meetings with people involved in different events made the conflict feel as if I were alive back then, but now I have witnessed a real protest stemming from the Troubles. It's amazing that some parts of this city manage to hide so much past suffering and violence from a tourist or new study abroad student until moments like this.

I step out of the crowd with my phone easily concealed. The Tony Taylor protesters continue their demonstration while I sneak around the back of the group and walk to the Peace Bridge, a causeway funded by the United Nations that connects the eastern and western banks across the River Foyle. There's nothing like a stroll over the water to help collect my thoughts after witnessing another act of dissent.

It was just last week that *Building Bridges* visited the Museum of Free Derry and Rossville Street, the location where fourteen Nationalist protesters were massacred by British paratroopers in the infamous Bloody Sunday of 1972. (Encyclopaedia Britannica Online Ed, Troubles, 2021) Sean and Gudrun led excursions to both of these sights; I saw bloody clothes, videos of clashes between civilians and military-police, and a memorial near Rossville Street that serves as ample reminder of past conflicts in Derry. Just when I assumed the legacy of the Troubles couldn't become any more real, I stumbled into a modern civil rights protest.

The sturdy white bridge railings and peaceful flow of dark blue water are calming forces after such a boisterous event. I am no expert in the case of Tony Taylor and cannot speak to the reality of his situation. However, I can say with certainty that today's Nationalist protest and those British flags from the trip home yesterday prove how tensions stemming from the Troubles are still present in 2017.

World history has never been more alive than in moments like those at the Guildhall courtyard. My initial interest in dissent outside of the USA is readily expanding beyond the American context. As I turn my eye to other parts of the globe like Derry, to places where a foreign people remain divided in their struggle for unity, the stark distinction between this current adventure and my freshman year begins to sink in: I'm more than three thousand miles from home.

Sean said it himself, that my classmates and I were to continue our *holistic* studies of the Irish people. Such diversity, the holism found in anything from hikes to protests, is proving to be an effective educational tool. These last two weeks began lifting the fog over my understanding of the Irish people, allowing sheer curiosity to shine on new aspects of this society I would've never encountered as a tourist. I can think of no more powerful method for engaging with the world than, well, literally going out there to find it.

My closed American perspective is finally starting to crack. Bias and disinterest in foreign societies are peeling like paint chips off an old monochrome drywall, and each subsequent day in Derry is a fresh coat of perspective with shades matching the Guildhall's stained glass windows. After completing an entire four weeks of holistic studies in the *Building Bridges* program, I begin to wonder if I'll ever view my own country the same way again.

Shouts for Tony Taylor recede into the distance as I gradually cross the Peace Bridge to Derry's eastern shore, or what's considered the Waterside. This part of town is known for its Protestant neighborhoods and schools, whereas the Guildhall and our dorms at Duncreggan are on the primarily Catholic western shore, or what's known as the Bogside. While my initial encounter with the eastern shore proved much quieter than the Tony Taylor demonstration, the Waterside eventually demonstrated how more than just Nationalist events take place in the small town of Derry.

BONFIRE

The sense of smell has to be one of the most powerful forces in the human body. Even without sight, sound, touch, or taste, the nose can instantly detect and analyze an object by the nature of its scent. Rotting eggs, blossoming flowers, a salty sea breeze; they plant distinct impressions up the nostrils. I'd even say some scents are unforgettable, nasal memories preserved for all time.

Perhaps most surprising are instances when one detects an unexpected smell—those moments when the other four senses suggest one reality and the nostrils beg to differ.

I am still a prisoner to my nose in Northern Ireland, no freer than in the States. I can (usually) choose how much Guinness rolls across the tongue or how long to run soft bits of Irish grass through my fingers. The nose, well, that's a different beast altogether.

The days are passing by at increasing speed and I'm almost at the midway point of *Building Bridges*. This is no time to start counting down the final hours, but there is some urgency to utilize my remaining time on this study abroad program. As such, I decided to take a night-time stroll to continue my exploration of Derry.

I'm barely across the Peace Bridge when my nose takes precedence over the pressure of a slight breeze, the murmur of my footsteps, and reflections from a pasty moon. It snatches my attention by detecting an odorous smoke, the kind of identifiable scent that implants itself inside the nasal cavity. I'm no stranger to this familiar smell after countless nights around campfires and indoor fires in our family's basement stove. However, as far as I can tell, there's no fire tonight, no camping allowed on the edge of the River Foyle.

I walk off the Peace Bridge in pursuit of this perplexing scent. A wind picks up from the south while I continue forward, blanketing the eastern shore with bursts of cool air as Derry descends into shadows. I make my way into the Waterside under the glare of musty lampposts and periodic slivers of light between clouds masking a waxing gibbous. Unfamiliar territory lies ahead, and there's still that pestering smell.

The streets glow bleakly on this peculiar summer night. I pass by closed shops and parked cars with no trace of their owners. The smokey scent strengthens as all thoughts of the River Foyle and Peace Bridge fade away to towering silhouettes of buildings and homes.

My nose guides me on a leash as the mystery scent intensifies. Chills from the river retreat to a rising air temperature and I wipe the slightest bit of perspiration from my forehead. The combination of these two senses is enough to spark my curiosity before I turn the corner a few blocks ahead and stop dead in my tracks. Another wipe of the brow and blink of the eyes do nothing to change the scene unfolding before me.

My dry lips mouth one single word: bonfire.

Hungry flames burn brightly in the vicinity of a nearby building and are fed by a collection of flammable objects. They eat up anything thrown in their path and finally offer closure to my nostrils' inquisition. My nasal irritation from the smoke is readily replaced by a tickling sensation in my eyes, and I can only offer so many scratches and rubs while stepping back to scrutinize this fire.

Piles of wooden objects lie scattered around its perimeter. I mistook similar heaps for trash during my first week in Derry. They seemed out of the ordinary, but nothing close to their apparent role in this bonfire. Several people crowd around the flames and every crackle illuminates even more strangers in the fire's orange glow. I need no mirror to be sure this bonfire colored my face like the moon, and images of the blaze drag me back to a recent *Building Bridges* lecture.

Tonight's bonfire burns on July 11th. To Unionists, today's date goes by the name of the "Eleventh Night" and is celebrated with bonfires in the streets across Northern Ireland. The flames serve a historical purpose, as they're lit just before July 12th, or "The Glorious Twelfth," a holiday that commemorates William of Orange's victory at the Battle of the Boyne, which occurred in 1690. Although they are meant to celebrate Unionist culture, some bonfires in Northern Ireland have been criticized for promoting "anti-social behavior." "Symbols of Irish Nationalism" have also been reportedly burned at past bonfires and efforts are being made to reduce this practice. (IrishCentral Staff, 2019)

I blink numbly at the pure size of the blaze and wilt with the knowledge that this event stands opposite to the Nationalist demands for Tony Taylor's release. This must be another shade of Derry's past that burns in fiery orange.

A few minutes' fixation is enough for me and my nostrils. I turn around and walk back quickly to Duncreggan as the smoky smell follows me through Waterside alleyways. Although the River Foyle eventually pops the bonfire's orange bubble, the flames still stalk my every move, plotting to yank me back to the blaze. I cross the Peace Bridge and find my way to the dorms at Duncreggan. My return is accompanied by smoky clothes, swirling thoughts, and the need to record my impressions.

Encountering a bonfire in the streets of Derry was a moving experience. I was immediately reminded of a book burning when I saw the large flames, not necessarily because there were books in the fire, but because I got a strange feeling from the entire scene. I find it concerning that one group of people might try to antagonize another by lighting fires in the streets, especially if those bonfires celebrate a legitimate historical event. How can the people here achieve full peace when groups (Protestant or Catholic, Unionist or Nationalist, doesn't matter) are still taking little jabs at the wounds of division that have plagued Derry? It is in the city's best interest to prevent events that could stir up conflict! I fear that true healing and forgiveness will be very difficult to achieve for the people of Derry so long as they continue with the fires, protests, and other reminders of the Troubles.

What started as a dense collection of Union Jacks after the Giant's Causeway just ended with a bonfire in Derry. While last November's protest in Philadelphia concerned recent events, the Tony Taylor protest and Unionist bonfire were modern demonstrations that took root in past conflicts like the Troubles. They both reaffirmed an unfortunate reality: the issues of Northern Ireland's past are still very much alive.

The last few weeks of holistic investigation proved that Irish dissent, like American, is two-sided. Tony Taylor and the bonfire are just two pieces of a larger plot that opened my eyes to opposing sides in a historical and cultural conflict. I am continually amazed by the people of Derry and find myself only one step closer to truly understanding their situation after experiencing the modern ghosts of past struggles. That being said, there remains much more to explore besides two live acts of dissent, and I eagerly await further scratches below the surface of this city's troubled past during my final weeks in Northern Ireland.

Despite the infamy of Bloody Sunday and general knowledge of paramilitary groups like the IRA and UVF, I would have never known of Derry had I not committed to *Building Bridges*. The city would have been nothing more than a foreign, unfamiliar place that is quite real to its people and their problems. I can only thank Ralph, Sean, and Gudrun for insisting that this international trip be a holistic tool for understanding the Irish people, not some superficial vacation.

How often do tourists go abroad and leave with nothing more than a naive perspective of the places they visit? People claim to be world travelers on Instagram after taking pictures of a foreign dish, exploring some tourist trap, and posing with a famous statue or natural wonder. Then it's off on their merry way, eager to explore the next location on a wash cycle of rinse and repeat.

There is nothing inherently wrong with tourism and I myself am no fantastic exemption from the above stereotype. From pints of Guinness to idyllic hikes, I will admit the majority of my experiences thus far in Derry have highlighted the most pleasing elements of this fantastic city. However, we must remember that solely skimming the surface of any culture, whether our own or another's, leaves us blind to its harsher realities.

With light comes darkness.

It's a question of whether we look in the shade.

The United States is by no means spared from superficial tourism. Regardless of where one comes from, I want to emphasize that we do not completely meet our duty as inhabitants of this planet when leaving a foreign place with nothing more than a black and white perspective of its reality. There is no substance in this type of colorblindness. To truly begin understanding a different culture, to actually claim any sort of appreciation for the complexities of an unfamiliar society, we must seek out every hue in the color palette of the peoples' experiences there. It is only then that the complete realities of life beyond our native shores come out from behind the curtain, exposing themselves for their beauty and struggles like the wizard in Victor Fleming's acclaimed *The Wizard of Oz.*

That smoky smell eventually compels me to abandon my journal and strip down for a shower. I hang my clothes by the window, quickly scuttle into the bathroom, and arrive at a frustrating conclusion. The stench clings even to my skin, determined to outdo my shivers on the frigid tile floor. I blast the scathing water and step eagerly into the spray, knowing all too well that the bonfire is much too far to warm me.

SANDINOS

I did not encounter any protests after the bonfire. To live abroad for a month is one thing; to witness more than two acts of foreign dissent is quite another. Despite all lingering tensions in Northern Ireland, the general public seems to have moved past the Troubles and I encountered a rather charming conclusion to *Building Bridges*.

I stroll through the city center on the final Sunday in Derry, excited for one last group event with Ralph, Sean, and Gudrun. I pass the Guildhall, turn onto Water Street, and look up at a black and gold sign on the bar to my left. It reads "Sandinos," a name which will forever have a special place in my heart.

Dancing skeletons greet me on several windows while I walk through the front doors. I enter the main bar under blue, purple, yellow, and red lights stretched across the ceiling. Protest flags from various dissent movements adorn every wall and fill in any space not already occupied by decorative trinkets and banners. My attention is easily snagged by pictures of deposed rulers, revolutionaries, and Augusto Sandino himself, the leader of a communist rebellion against United States involvement in Nicaragua during the early 20th century.

Wooden tables are scattered all about the cramped seating area and Sandinos is already near full capacity. I walk up to the front bar and find decorative taps for classic Irish brews like Guinness, Smithwicks, and Harp while the refrigerators are lined with Derry specialties like Dopey Dick. It's hard to go wrong with almost any of them.

Sandinos is a popular spot on late Sunday afternoons for its unique musical traditions. Live music is commonplace in any Irish pub, and Sandinos is renowned for its Sunday night music sessions starting at 17:30. The bar has no room for dancing on the first floor, but that never stops me from enjoying some sweet Irish melodies with more than a pint or two.

I take a seat alongside Ralph, Sean, Gudrun, and other Temple students sitting in the far back corner. Though not occupied by locals, the Temple section made itself known after four consecutive Sunday visits. My table is in close proximity to a majority of the musicians and offers a view of the entire scene at Sandinos.

We collect our drinks as the performers arrive one by one, adorning their instrument of choice and receiving the first of many rounds on the house. They speak hardly a word and get straight to work, playing hundreds of Irish songs from memory. Fiddle, pipes, banjo, mandolin, penny whistle, and the traditional Bodhrán drum are the means for tonight's performance.

I've listened to a good many artists so far in my life, but there's nothing quite like live Irish music, in Northern Ireland, while holding a Guinness.

The musicians perform a collection of different songs before pausing for their first break. My peers and I exchange looks of confusion as they retreat out of the spotlight and sit in prolonged silence. Although I've been to a month's worth of Sunday night music sessions, that doesn't mean there's no room left for surprises.

"Listen," says Sean after someone mentions the stoppage. "This is no ordinary break. Quiet down now and see what you can hear."

I look away from the musicians when an older Irish gentleman raises slowly from his seat. He stands just beside the bar, leans to one side, and has gelled gray hair that contrasts with his plaid shirt and blue dress pants. I would have passed him by as a stranger on any normal night at Sandinos.

He begins to sing after a moment's pause. Customers set down their drinks and chatter vanishes out of respect for his song. The man muses in a non-metrical meter, captivating the audience with changing dynamics and occasional pauses that suit the natural rhythm of his lyrics. He recites his story without staring at any one person in particular as almost all the instrumentalists remain quiet and out of sight. It sounds like he's singing in Gaelic, the native language of the Gaelic people of Ireland and Scotland.

The singer projects a degree of casualness not found in any of my previous experiences with concert band and orchestra. I cannot understand a word he's saying, but as I lean forward with other Temple students to soak in every verse of his song, the man still finds a way to connect with us like we speak his language. The music is his to sing and share.

"What's the song about?" I whisper to Sean.

He grins and takes a sip of his drink.

"This type of Gaelic singing is an old tradition here at Sandinos, not done every Sunday, but a special part of the music hour. It's hard to exactly tell with all the background noise, but I can say from past experience that he's educating us about Irish life of olden times, describing the history, culture, and music of our people. Quite fascinating, no?"

Fiddlers contribute to the melody as the man approaches what must be a more familiar section of his song. Some patrons also begin singing a few lines before the tempo gradually slows. They all drop out in unison as the old man reaches his final note, finishes the song with a triumphant exclamation, and concludes the entire piece with a nod of his head.

He immediately receives a chorus of applause and whistling from all corners of the bar. The man shakes a few hands and returns to his seat before queuing the musicians to pick up their instruments. They quickly start another fast-paced tune after tending to the half-full glasses on the table in front of them.

"So," says Gudrun in her slight German accent, "what do you all think about coming back to Derry and Europe? Is this something that would interest you in the future?"

"Absolutely," I reply. "I think it's fair to say that more than a few of us have caught the European travel bug. After a performance like that, I'm eager to come back to Derry, visit the rest of Ireland, maybe explore other parts of Europe, who knows!"

We all clink glasses for the traditional Irish cheer of *Sláinte!* before long, satiating sips of our drinks. I can feel the Guinness warm my entire body while thoughts of the future start tumbling into mind. Though I have no computer at Sandinos, there's nothing like a well-recorded mental note for later.

Building Bridges was not solely an academic adventure. Everything, between the walks, lectures, gatherings at Sandinos, guest speakers, literature sessions, and pure exploration, made this experience abroad much more than any college course I've taken so far. I never imagined living in Northern Ireland for a month, and if I'm sure of one thing, it's that I'm eager to study abroad again while at Temple.

The storms surrounding my introduction to college now seem far behind as I take the last sip of my Guinness and rest the decorative glass down on the table beside my new friends and colleagues. As I stare at the old man across the bar, I can only reflect on how much this trip made me want to travel and explore the world *with purpose*. A *Building Bridges*-style education built on the uniqueness I found with Ralph last fall; no public school history class ever offered a chance to hike the pastures, cliff sides, and beaches in the land I was studying; no university course of mine ever urged students to check out different cultural establishments and listen to local musicians right down the street from campus on a daily basis; not even *Dissent in America* involved the same amount of in-depth and in-person experience to match *Building Bridges*.

This summer reaffirmed my interest in dissent and fostered a curiosity for dissecting foreign societies. My experiences with *Building Bridges* led to new passions for world history, language, literature, and nature; most importantly, studying abroad in Northern Ireland ensured that holistic educational methods would remain influential in my studies and life after Derry.

The final, foamy sip of my Guinness signified more than just the need for another drink. It completed my transformation from a lonely, disillusioned freshman to a student of dissent in Northern Ireland. I arrived in Derry with a relatively closed perspective and now seek to become nothing less than a world citizen after combining my American upbringing with the experiences of a student in Europe.

We all leave pieces of ourselves in the foreign places we visit, traces of our identities that will always belong to the people we met there and experiences we had. Although I will always be American in my travels abroad, that will not stop me (nor should it) from falling into the arms of foreign cultures in my pursuit of an international perspective. This trip to Northern Ireland was just one piece of my metamorphosis throughout college, and while my interest in avoiding a limited perspective continued well beyond Derry, I look back on this study abroad experience and my leap of faith on *Building Bridges* with more than overwhelming satisfaction.

Whether you've spent years abroad or never left your home country, I urge you to consider this month in Derry as proof that engagement with the outside world is an absolutely wonderful and productive aspect of the human experience. *Building Bridges* begged me to ask myself the following questions, and I similarly pose them to you:

How often do you look outside your comfort zone and seek a holistic view of your interests, goals, and challenges?

Have you ever tried to change your perspective by looking overseas at foreign ideas?

Do you have any bias against perspectives from other places in the world?

Are you willing to take international opinions and mindsets into consideration when making important decisions?

If you haven't traveled abroad before, are you ready to take that leap of faith?

Passion and dissent were the keys to my personal development up to the start of *Building Bridges*, and as I wish for one additional sip of my Guinness in Sandinos, I offer another key to navigating change in young adulthood: holistic international education.

This third tool is my most powerful takeaway from studying abroad and plays a crucial role in my life to this day. The hikes, lectures, museum visits, city tours, and dissent, along with the relationships I developed with my peers and instructors, have kept me in contact with life outside North America since 2017. The notion of holism redefined my approach towards education, left me with a determination to find well-roundedness in the grand scheme of whatever I do, and forever changed my trajectory after that summer abroad. While only you can decide how much international influence belongs in your decision making process, I only ask that you give foreign perspectives a chance. You never know where they might take you.

This is neither my last European trip nor my final Guinness with the people who made it possible. I've metaphorically built bridges across the Atlantic with Ralph and company, and as I dream of flying home over ours, the only unresolved matter is what I'm actually going to do *after* Derry. I studied abroad to find clarity regarding my choice of major, and unfortunately leave Northern Ireland with no particular conviction for one academic program at Temple or another. There must be a degree path or certain combination of major and additional coursework to meet my interests in international education, dissent, music, and the never-ending list of new interests and passions from this summer.

A solution has to be out there, and I just have yet to find it.

I would eventually choose and commit to one particular undergraduate program after returning to Philadelphia in Fall 2017. My final choice still intrigues good friends to this day. Though it's incredibly tempting to discuss such a decision after Derry, I cannot waste this opportunity for additional suspense and look forward to discussing my major in due time.

I will offer the following clue: my most important experiences after Derry had nothing to do with Temple University. After investigating dissent with Ralph over the past year, fate put me on a path to reunite with one of my earliest passions from high school and assimilate in a "foreign" culture unknown to almost all people. But, please, I can't get ahead of myself, for there are still a few moments left to enjoy in Sandinos.

As I glance out past the old man, looking through those dancing skeletons on the front window and over the hedges across the street, I can see the Peace Bridge standing tall over the River Foyle. The water is now a shimmering blue with reflections from the descending sun and flows steadily forward as I prepare for closure with the section of my life called Derry, Northern Ireland.

The conversation among those remaining at the end of the music session transitions to favorite moments from *Building Bridges*. One such memory comes from the musical analysis of *The Town I Loved So Well*, a song written by Phil Coulter and released by The Dubliners during the Troubles in 1973. As our group gets up to leave Sandinos, ready to call it on this final Sunday night in Derry, I can already sense inspiration from the title of Coulter's song at the conclusion of my final journal entry like the taste of Guinness still lingering on my tongue.

I certainly do love Derry, and while my pen may fall silent on the town for now, I eagerly await our reunion in years to come.

ICE HOCKEY
OFFICIATING

HARVARD

Life is a grandfather clock. It ticks steadily forward, accompanying us from morning to night. The onlooker may fascinate themselves with its facade of sculpted wood, beveled glass, and a familiar minute hand that conducts like the most eloquent maestro. Yet a beautiful appearance conceals the machinery of time, a collection of gears, pulleys, and springs which lurk in the shadows, out of sight.

At the heart of any grandfather clock bobs a single pendulum, the steadying force that synchronizes the entire machine with the rest of the world. The pendulum swings periodically, guaranteeing its displacement to one side as much as a return to the other. This time engine is steadfast and resolute; scrutinize it as you wish, but there's no denying its harmonic rhythm that will outlive the both of us.

My pendulum reached peak displacement at the end of *Building Bridges*. Years of PMEA festivals, artistic dissent, and exposure to traditional Irish music were a full swing towards my passion for music. While I likely looked at digital time during my final moments in Derry, my pendulum had new plans for a downward arc.

It was time to reunite with an old friend: ice hockey.

I recall occasions from my playing days with Rinaldi where I wondered if my involvement in our sport would eventually end. The conclusion of high school left me determined to feed my passion for hockey, and though it was unclear how that might occur, young Adam was convinced he could find a way.

Ice hockey did have a minor though insignificant role in the struggles of freshman year. My first few months at Temple fostered no interest in joining our club ice hockey team, and I left for Derry wondering if I may never again skate so frequently as I did in high school.

My grandfather clock would have none of that. It booked me a one-way ticket at the end of *Building Bridges* to somewhere distinctly separate from the home I left behind just one month ago. Each passing minute on that flight back to Philadelphia energized my pendulum in an entirely new swing, imparting momentum that would lead me to assume the role of a character I often befriended back in high school.

The next few years after Derry were facilitated, if not dominated, by my love for ice hockey officiating.

The refereeing community is removed from mainstream society; I'd argue most Americans know more about Ireland than officiating, let alone for a sport like ice hockey. We officials are those mechanical components in the grandfather clock, locked away behind fancy engravings and distractions while simultaneously essential to the entire body's functionality. Strangers are often surprised when I mention my passion for this nontraditional activity, and my message to them is always the same: it is the best side job I could have ever asked for. Refereeing ice hockey would offer unimaginable opportunities in the more recent years of my life, and while I take pride in my craft, I must confess a rather uninspiring beginning to my officiating career.

The time seemed right for finding a part-time job in late 2013. While there was plenty of work available at food and department stores, I was actively playing for travel and high school hockey teams and could not commit to regularly scheduled positions on the weekends.

My pivot away from the traditional job market led me to the one place I knew best. There were always ice hockey referees in the rink, and my dad, a golf player himself, often mentioned how he made good money as a caddy in high school and college. He was no official, but I liked the analogue between his former work and my potential to pick up some spare cash as a referee.

I needed a source of income, and as Rinaldi did in 2009, I just said screw it, *why not try.*

I registered with USA Hockey, the primary governing body for youth ice hockey in the United States, and joined a community of roughly twenty thousand officials across the nation. My first season was rough, yielding something close to a dozen games. Many took place at unfathomable hours, and my parents can tell you fond memories of waking up at 4:30 a.m. to drive me to my 5:30 a.m. spring in-house assignments. We've joked about the subject on many occasions, and I'll use this opportunity to say *thank you* once again.

Those games were made even less desirable with poor pay and constant indecision regarding my potential for attractive assignments in the future. Although I was fortunate to officiate a U8 in-house championship in the spring of 2014, it was not clear if I would ever do something beyond a dozen introductory games. The retention of first-year youth ice hockey officials hovers around 50 percent and I took part in that coin toss.

Fast forward to July 2018, one year after Derry and just weeks before my junior year of college, and I'm waiting outside a coaches room in the Bright-Landry Hockey Center, home of

Harvard University's NCAA D1 college hockey program. I'm one of twenty participants waiting for my exit interview after the first ever College Hockey Officiating Experience Camp led by NHL Linesman Brian Murphy. He and BJ Ringrose, Manager of USA Hockey's Officiating Education Program, complete the interview before mine while I, reflecting on three days at Harvard, stare at the empty ice surface.

I hardly thought my first trip to Boston would be to learn from some of the best ice hockey officials in the world. "Murph" invited guest speakers representing the NHL, AHL, Olympics, and the highest levels of collegiate hockey. I even met the legend himself: NHL Referee Wes McCauley.

I spent three days studying videos, receiving game feedback, and gathering insight from every officiating teacher and guest speaker. The first time I learned from an NHL official was at the 2016 Atlantic District Officiating Camp, a week-long developmental program led by NHL referee and Philadelphia native Ian Walsh. District Camp was the first experience that opened my eyes to opportunities far beyond those 5:30 a.m. assignments. Ian was an incredible teacher, and although attending his camp was impressive after only three years as an official, I assumed it was the peak of my career. I liked officiating but was just some kid playing average ice hockey in the Philadelphia suburbs. If you had told me I was to follow up Ian's camp with Murph's first ever college-preparatory program and a firm handshake with Wes McCauley, I would've never believed you.

Yet here I am in Harvard's home rink, dressed in a dark blue collared shirt, black tie, and tan khaki pants. While I would usually experience waves of social anxiety before such an important meeting, my heart rate hovers just above normal and I'm ready to face the music. The saying goes that one should "leave it all on the ice" and that's exactly what I did over the past three days.

My ears perk up at a clicking sound and I turn to see the coaches' room door thrust wide open. It immediately reminds me of my memories from PMEA, and the only question remaining is if this interview will be like my first or second sight-reading.

"Hey Adam, feel free to take a seat," says Murph. He gestures at the empty chair across the table from him and BJ. I cross the room and sit down, running one hand along my tie and the other through my hair.

One of NHL officials' most impressive attributes is their laser-like intensity about anything related to ice hockey. Ian Walsh first proved this in 2016 and the pattern persisted upon meeting other NHL officials like Murph and Wes McCauley. Few people understand the dynamics of ice hockey better than the referees and linesmen working the highest level of competition in the world. Their focus and intellectual appreciation of the game, ability to dissect every play and conversation, and capability to make thousands of decisions per minute in an incredibly fast sport are, among a great many other things, what makes them NHL officials. They prove their qualifications every game and carry that intense mentality into the classroom. Such is the advantage of having them as a teacher.

Murph begins our conversation with the predictable question in his north-eastern accent.

"How did you feel about camp, both your individual performance and the activities themselves?"

"I had a fantastic time," I respond. "'Never thought I'd be able to skate up here at Harvard with some of the best in the business. I made some mistakes but learned a lot from you all along the way."

Murph nods. "It's rewarding to help officials like yourself and better our community. I do think you did a great job at camp, and before we officially end, I want to reiterate a few key ideas that will be invaluable in your career."

"Number one," he begins, "always remember that ice hockey officiating is an *art*, not a science. There is no formula to perfection."

"Secondly, successful officials build and maintain relationships. This applies both on and off the ice with players, coaches, and certainly with other officials. Good relationships build trust, and we use that trust to gain the confidence of all game participants."

"On a final note," he says, "never forget that your journey to this camp is just where officiating has taken you so far. We're all part of an amazing sport, and I look forward to seeing where it takes you in future seasons. Please keep in touch and take care."

"Thank you Murph, that means the world."

I shake hands with him and BJ before standing up and reentering the crisp air of the Bright-Landry Hockey Center.

I started officiating a mere five years ago to pick up cash. My first games felt more or less like chores, certainly disconnected from my intense passion for playing the game I loved. Though my interest in refereeing certainly increased after the Atlantic District Camp, my transformation into a true ice hockey official was greatly accelerated by the College Hockey Officiating Experience Camp.

Brian Murphy became my officiating analogue of Ralph Young. This was of little surprise, for Murph inherited Ralph's role as instructor and coach for something other than dissent and forever changed my outlook on officiating. After learning from Murph at Harvard, my job as a referee was no longer just some simple passion on the weekends, but rather an art form that depended on my ability to build and maintain relationships. The best teachers present their pupils with as many questions as answers and Murph was no exception to this rule. I left our interview as his student, so sure of what we discussed in camp while equally curious to explore his teachings in my upcoming season and junior year of college.

The question of how Murph's officiating guidance would affect the 2018-2019 season answers itself in a matter of months. What goes up must come down, and just as the grandfather clock's pendulum descends from high to low, so too does my trip up north to Harvard follow with an excursion to a unique university down south. I'm taking a weekend trip to the world of officiating, preparing to explore an unfamiliar part of the United States where I never knew hockey even existed. My destination lies down below the Mason-Dixon line, and as I pack my gear with an unfamiliar referee from Philadelphia, the time is ripe for putting Murph's lessons to the test.

Liberty University, here I come.

SIX FOR SIX

"Brock, pass me another mango. Suckers are too damn good."

Mike Delfin steps into the driver's seat of his black SUV and slides on a pair of brown-tinted sunglasses. I dig deep into the passenger seat cup holder and discover one last pack of Hi-Chew candies among a collection of torn wrappers and crinkled paper. Delfin accepts my offering and revs the engine. We pull out of a hotel parking lot in Lynchburg, Virginia with ref bags packed into the trunk and bellies full of chicken sandwiches. The sky is a soft, delicate blue as I roll down my window to feel the breeze in early October 2018.

A full night's work awaits us. The campus of Liberty University is just out of sight as we enter the highway and chart a course for LaHaye Ice Center, home of the Liberty Flames ACHA ice hockey program. The ACHA, or American Collegiate Hockey Association, is a college athletics organization that draws club hockey teams from universities and colleges across the United States. Programs compete in either Division 1, 2, or 3, and while the quality of club ice hockey greatly varies from one school to another, the Liberty Flames boast some of the best men's and women's teams in the entire ACHA.

Tonight's assignment is none other than the Friday night special: the D1 Men's at 7:00 p.m. I've heard many stories about the D1 Men's games in Liberty's LaHaye Ice Center, legends ranging from midnight games to barn-busting fights, insanely large crowds to teddy bear tosses. This is also Delfin's first trip down south to Liberty in more than ten years of officiating. Last we heard, the D1 Men's team is nationally ranked within the top ten ACHA programs this season and shows no signs of deviating from that position. I know nothing about their opponent, though it really might make no difference.

Liberty is a powerhouse.

There's a saying in sports about making it "to the show," or to the elite levels of the game we all love. As the LaHaye Ice Center comes into view, glistening like a silver spoon in the late-day sun, Delfin and I exchange glances that conceal what must be the same apprehensions. Our upcoming assignment is no ordinary game and I have no doubt that this is to be my biggest challenge as an official to date. I am a college student refereeing college students, a young buck thrown into the officiating world with a veteran like Delfin who has yet to encounter a game like tonight's.

I pop another Hi-Chew knowing that this will be my first true test of Murph's teachings after Harvard. The relationships I build will be critical in determining this game's outcome, for they will either cultivate rapport between myself and all other participants or leave me incapable of handling any major challenges. Though I've bonded with my fellow Philadelphia-based referee and former collegiate ice hockey player during the last six hours of a car trip down south, I don't know what to expect of Delfin on the ice. No clearer are the future dynamics between us, our partners, and everyone that awaits our arrival in LaHaye.

I sit on the edge of my car seat with all sorts of officiating legends running through my head, knowing all too well that we will make our own story at Liberty tonight.

***

I finish tightening both skates as excitement permeates the foundation of LaHaye Ice Center. The official's locker room sits at the base of the volcano that is this rink in southern Virginia; an ocean of lava waits only a short walk away, ready to smother me at first chance. Volcanic pressure grows as each passing second only brings us closer to an eruption at 7:00 p.m.

Delfin sits to my left, wiping some cleaner off his helmet visor while Mason Riley sits across from the both of us. Riley's the third Philadelphia-based official at Liberty this weekend and drove down separately. The three of us will work tonight's game in the four-official system with a partner from the Liberty area. Delfin and I are referees, meaning we wear the orange arm bands and focus on penalties and goals, while Riley and his partner are linesmen who concern themselves with game mechanics such as face-offs, icings, and offsides.

Some like to make fun of the tension between referees and linesmen and incite drama about one role or another, questioning why someone is this and not that. The positions are distinctly different, but the singular fact remains that all officials, especially in the four-official system, depend on each other to properly manage hockey games.

We succeed or fail as a unit. End of story.

I rise from my seat after zipping up my referee sweater and join Delfin, Riley, and the other linesman by the door.

"Alright boys, let's go!" cheers Mike as we all bump fists and slap our patches into place, one of many well-preserved pre-game traditions. The scorekeeper opens the door and we walk out together into the heart of LaHaye.

We begin a long, straight march underneath the stands. Our officiating team strides in quiet unison, a silence contrasting greatly from volcanic rumblings up above. I turn right at the end of the hallway and look out into the rink. Fans dressed in Liberty jerseys, sweatshirts, and T-shirts litter the seats all around us. They rock the building's foundation with blow horns, whistles, microphones, and cowbells. Members of Liberty's film crew circle the crowd and are illuminated by the brightly colored scoreboard shining above center ice.

The scorekeeper opens a door to the rink. "Okay guys, it's all you."

I look over at Delfin, get a nod in return, and sprint out onto the ice.

Our entrance was surreal. Never before have I seen different shades of purple, red, and blue parade across my black, white, and orange jersey. Never before have I looked up into the stands to see more than five thousand fans jostling for position around one single rink. Never before have my deep, jagged cuts into the ice been drowned out by explosive commentary from a fiery announcer rallying his crowd.

Then again, what should I have expected? Never before had I been to any place quite like Liberty University.

"Laddieeees aaaaand gentlemeeennnn, welcome to the LaHaye Ice Center!" booms through the dark atmosphere after all four of us meet by the scorekeeper.

"Let's give it up for your LIBERTYYYYY FLAAAAAAAAMMES!!!"

The D1 Men's team bursts out of an inflatable tunnel. Their entrance is accompanied by smoke cannons and fanatical shrieks from the crowd. Liberty players circle their defensive zone and the goalies enter the ice with their mascot, a flightless bird with a Flames jersey and no skating skills whatsoever.

"Hey Delfy," I chirp, "I think you need some lessons from that bird. Could really help us out tonight."

Riley leans over. "Eh, you too Brocker! He's putting you both to shame."

"Alright you two, if anyone's talking shit, it's me, the crew boss," asserts Delfin, standing tall on both skates.

"Not so!" Riley and I can agree on that one.

The house lights reappear and we refasten our helmets after the anthem and pre-game prayer, a unique Liberty tradition. Delfin presents me with a puck from the scorekeeper and rallies our crew one last time.

"Let's go boys, best team on the ice!"

We bump fists again and take our respective positions.

I skate to center ice with the puck in hand as the depths of LaHaye begin to rumble. My heart pounds when players from both teams line up for our opening draw. I point to both goalies, assuring that each is ready, and then confirm our start time with the scorekeeper. LaHaye is on the edge of rupture as players on both benches begin banging their sticks with the support of five thousand fans. I can hardly hear my own voice, let alone my thoughts.

I've come quite a ways from those early 5:30 a.m. starts. I look around the rink with my eyes wide open at the sight of so many cameras, lights, announcers, players, coaches, fans, staff, and my partners. They all await that significant drop, my first act as a referee, and the beginning of our Friday night rodeo at Liberty. This moment marks the beginning of all in-game interactions, the first step toward achieving the trust that Murph so fervently championed through proper relationships. I've already built some rapport with Delfin and Riley, and the real test of our communication and coordination is about to begin.

A sharp blast of my whistle readies both centers and I fling the polished, frozen puck down onto the blue center ice dot. The players pounce, I take my first stride, and the machinery of ice hockey lurches into motion.

***

I am continually fascinated by the negative correlation between concentration and memory. I often fail to remember exactly what happened or what I might have done after moments of the most intense focus; for example, there were times after my PMEA auditions and former games as a player and official where I struggled to recall specific memories and discern a clear picture of what just happened. I believe this is likely a consequence of "living in the moment," for the act of doing does not always necessitate the formation of memory.

My recollections from this Liberty game are like puffs of smoke: numerous, scattered, adrift in the nearest breeze. Although I remember sweating under the bright lights and watching Liberty dominate the first forty minutes of play, there are no specific details from the first two periods of this game which left the same kind of impression as those from the third. Unless I truly go senile, as close friends say I already have, I will never forget the third period from this Friday night showdown.

The four of us stand in the referee's crease and take a breather during the first of three television stoppages in the third period. Liberty broadcasts their D1 Men's team on ESPN+ in Virginia, as if there weren't enough eyes watching us already. There's only five minutes or so left in this game and Liberty has a commanding lead. It took little time for them to dominate their opponent, and in a competition with such lopsided skills, it is imperative for the diligent official to be extra cautious regarding injury and aggression. Hockey is an emotional sport, and noncompetitive games such as this one run the risk of getting out of hand when emotions become inflamed.

Delfin skates to my side at the break's conclusion.

"We're reffing a hell of a game here Brock, be wary of any unnecessary shit. Keep crushing it."

"You got it Delfy, let's send 'er home."

Riley skates to a faceoff dot in Liberty's offensive zone while Delfin proceeds to the other side of the goal in end-zone position. I start the line change procedure and point to Riley after its conclusion. He blows his whistle, lines the boys up for the resumption of play, and drops the puck.

Riley begins skating backward out of the zone as players ambush that black piece of rubber. I maintain my position above the blue line, etching small circles and figure-eights into the ice while Liberty gains possession below the goal line. Delfin maintains command in the corner as I continue scanning the zone, looking for all the sparks that could light the fuse to this powder keg in LaHaye.

Liberty's opponents finally gain control of the puck and wrap it behind their net. I take note of an opposing winger as the puck travels up the boards to a Liberty defender in front of the visiting team's bench. Liberty's opponent makes a beeline after the puck, and in one of many moments where the human body proves superior to the mind, the hairs fling up on the back of my neck.

The winger wallops the Liberty defender after he releases a pass. It is a clean but crushing hit, and the defender falls like a bird shot out of the sky. He lands right in front of the opponent's bench and lays still, devoid of life. I can hardly react to this event before other Liberty forwards change course and teleport at light speed to exactly where you'd think: right at the guy who just annihilated their buddy. One by one, the Liberty players pounce on their enemy to make him pay for such a punishing hit. Their actions then draw in more opponents who rally around their lone teammate in front of their bench.

My right arm flies up to signal a penalty at the first sign of mischief, but it's already too late: we have a fight on our hands. The Huskies championship was nothing short of a shitshow, but while I thought I saw the uglier side of hockey come out during games in high school, I was in for a whole new spectacle at Liberty.

The linesmen can hardly address the altercation before all ten skaters on the ice, excluding the goalies, become combatants in a cage match. The stage is set, lights focused, bell rung, rules abandoned. Delfin and I move in to block any additional players from each bench who may want to join in the chaos. As referees, we usually watch fights and record notes for penalties while the linesmen break up the combatants.

The real eruption of volcano LaHaye was waiting for this particular moment. The full crowd of more than five thousand mutes my ears, cutting off a crucial sense as I try to process the ongoing carnage. My arm remains high in the air and grows stiff as the spectators lap up every second of the fight. Their boys are skilled at more than just playing.

It takes bitter persuasion and encouragement before our officiating team reduces the fight to six players. Two occupy Mason in a tussle on the ice while his partner holds back a pair near the bench. I watch the third duo, keeping a safe distance with the intent to act when either combatant gains too great of an advantage over the other. Delfin remains positioned between both benches and chirps going back and forth between both teams. Riley eventually separates the last two combatants and hastily escorts them off the ice. Delfin and I proceed slowly to the scorekeeper's box and watch both teams in the event that the slugfest resumes.

I acknowledge the scorekeeper and then turn to Mike.

"Well, that was fun. What do we think about those penalties Delfin?"

The fans continue cheering wildly, rocking LaHaye's core and banging so loud on the scorekeeper's box that we have to huddle close together.

"Don't you know what they say Brock?"

"Enlighten me."

"Easy," he replies, "keep it simple, stupid."

"Okay, we had a big hit up top and two guys who instantly began the fight. Grew to ten players but we really ended up with six, agree with me there?"

"Absolutely."

I look down at the scoresheet and then back up to Mike. Both Riley and his partner now join us.

"How about six DQ's then? Six for six, like a fast-food combo or some shit. Keeps it simple with the most important fighters."

He looks over to both linesmen and they nod in agreement.

"I like it. Simple and effective."

We turn to the scorekeeper and explain the penalty assessment. DQ stands for "Disqualification" and includes a five-minute major penalty, removal of the offending player from the game, and at least a one-game suspension, though this can differ by league, conference, combination with other penalties, and etc. An equal number of DQ's to each team means all the penalties, considered "coincident" in this situation, negate one another and no time is displayed on the scoreboard. (Piotrowski, Halpin, and Stubbeman, 2018)

All six players are removed from the game and our end result is just like we started: five-on-five hockey. Delfin and I check the scoresheet and plan our next steps with Mason and the other linesman. We explain the penalty assessment to both captains, work out the logistics of resuming play, and line up the boys for another draw.

Six for six, not a bad deal after all.

This first game at Liberty was one of the most unique assignments in my officiating career. It offered me an opportunity to handle a cage match with five thousand fans or lose my composure, fail to protect the players, and be unable to respect our great game with proper penalty assessment. Fights will always be a part of ice hockey and on the long list of officiating duties. However, witnessing Rinaldi's battles in high school was quite different from tonight's challenge to officiate AND manage a fight AND decide the consequences in its aftermath AND remain collected through the whole ordeal in an inaudible building like LaHaye.

This game confirmed some of Murph's most pivotal guidance—the notion that officiating is all about relationships between individuals and a group. I used to think of relationships with my partners as one-dimensional, limited to the few moments in a game where our coordination mattered most. Tonight's rodeo at Liberty proved this wrong in its entirety with dynamics of all different sorts: Delfin and I when traveling, bullshitting with Mason, assessing penalties, working together with our partners during an incredible fight. Our dialogue, bonds, support, and jokes shaped our relationships and facilitated success.

I never knew I would skate with Delfin and Riley at Liberty University, let alone referee their Men's D1 team and manage a gigantic line brawl. This story is but a paragraph in the encyclopedia of officiating, a sampling from the many unforeseeable developments in my officiating career. While Murph may not have known I'd be making a trip to Liberty, he was certainly right in stating that our sport would take me *somewhere*.

This first night at LaHaye is my personal testament to the transformative power of officiating. My side-job for picking up extra cash on the weekends took me places far beyond my wildest dreams after I invested the necessary time, energy, and effort to improve my skills and build rapport with different facets of the hockey community. A commitment to officiating leads some to incredible levels of competition in the NCAA, international hockey with the IIHF, or professional leagues like the NHL or AHL. In my case, officiating gave me the experience to travel south, be an integral part of a D1 Men's ACHA game at Liberty, and give back to the game I loved as a kid. I still officiate to this day and look forward to the next steps in my journey as a referee, whenever and wherever they may be.

Despite my initial thoughts to the contrary, Murph's teachings and emphasis on relationships still apply in those early morning in-house games and at the lowest levels of competitive ice hockey. As I join my officiating teammates in post-game festivities after this Friday night special at LaHaye, my mind wanders back in time to those introductory assignments where relationships were of fundamental importance to others besides myself. I remember there is indeed another who learned to sink or swim through early morning games and building relationships: my brother.

WATCH THIS

The front door closes behind our officiating crew as we stroll into a tavern in downtown Lynchburg. We have the whole posse of refs together and are swapping our place of work at LaHaye for some Friday night mischief at the bar.

A collective post-game scent marks off our territory as we make ourselves at home. It's the smell of a long night's work, and there's nothing more fitting for afterward than a brewsky or two with the boys. We sit down at the nearest available table and immediately order drinks. I glance over to see newly arrived pitchers of Bud Light in front of Delfin and Riley.

"Hey guys, I thought we were drinking beer tonight, not water."

"Screw off Brocker, the price is right and so is the brew," barks a fiery Riley, already licking his lips after sips from a frosted glass of that light, frothy liquid.

Delfin turns my way. "C'mon Brock, what are you now, a beer snob? What did you get?"

I show them both the logo on my glass. "European, best choice I made all night."

"Agh!" exclaims Riley. "You can't use that crap to beat a deal like these pitchers!"

We exchange a few laughs before another truckload of Bud Light arrives at the table. Delfin then sits up in his chair with his glass raised high.

"Honestly guys, I think we did a great job tonight, six for six and all. No better way to celebrate than with the boys and some drinks."

His comment is followed by more than one round of cheers. I can only think I'm living by Murph's wisdom once again, developing my relationships with officiating teammates off the ice. The conversation then takes a more serious tone after Delfin mentions his young son who just began playing ice hockey. He stares at his glass with a glossy look in his eyes.

"My boy really loves it. I can see it each day when he puts on his gear and gets excited for games."

Delfin looks up from his beer and grins like a parent who eagerly awaits the surprises his children will offer the world.

"I personally couldn't have asked for a better way to give back to hockey by refereeing and having my kid play. I hope that he'll consider officiating with his old man one day. Never know where this sport might take us."

I sip my drink and watch bubbles slowly rise in the amber-colored lager. Delfin just connected officiating with family, something never specifically mentioned at Harvard. Could it be that refereeing also improves these types of relationships? If hockey creates family on the ice, then it might just strengthen families too. While the conversation shifts to another topic, my thoughts drift back to memories where family was at the center of officiating.

***

Desmond Brock follows me into Rink 3 at the Ice Works Skating Complex in Aston, PA. The side door sticks open behind us on this Saturday morning in November 2017, the season before Murph's Harvard camp.

My younger brother and I share a variety of passions. We both love ice hockey, play clarinet and saxophone, and goof off in our free time. Though our interests somewhat diverged after I entered college, the list of similarities grew in 2016 from another item: ice hockey officiating.

"Adam, what level are we reffing again?" Des walks by my side and carries his camouflage equipment bag, the same one I used many years ago.

"Pretty sure it's U12 in-house."

I point up at the rink clock. "Twenty minutes till we're on at 8:00 a.m. Let's get dressed and do this thing."

We suit up in matching jerseys and hit the ice, a pair of brothers living the dream. Unlike the D1 Men's at Liberty, we are officiating this game in the two-official system and carry out the duties of both referees and linesmen. This is Des' second season, and although he's already officiated a few games this fall, today's assignment is his first in over a month.

I use our games together to help Des develop his refereeing skills. Experienced officials are teachers to players, coaches, and new officials at the lowest levels, and there's no one I'd rather instruct than my off-the-wall, batshit crazy brother. He has a zest for life and it translates on the ice.

"Remember Des, checking and other types of illegal contact are not permitted in U12." Rule refreshers before each game are never a bad idea.

"And we're doing automatic off-sides?" he asks.

Off-sides occurs when an attacking team does not properly cross the blue line when entering their offensive zone.

"Exactly right," I reply, happy to see he's checking all the boxes. "You ready?"

"It's been a while," he shrugs, "but yeah, I am."

We briefly greet both sets of coaches and I hand him a puck for the opening faceoff.

"Let's make sure to communicate if anything weird happens, ok?"

"You got it."

He skates out to center ice and adjusts his pants along the way (looking to prevent them from falling down *again* during play, though that's a story for another time). Des points to both goalies, signals the scorekeeper, and confidently blasts his whistle. He then drops the puck and begins this Saturday morning showdown with two referee brothers on patrol once again.

The match starts without a hitch. Des' full strides across the ice and correct applications of the youth rules show few signs of a month's rust. We make it through half the game without any strange occurrences, but if I know one thing about officiating, then it's to expect the unexpected. Deceivingly innocent moments often produce the oddest possible situations; I don't care what level I'm working because there's always room for surprises.

I hover just above the blue line towards the end of the 2nd period while Des watches play in the end zone corner. He moves up and down along the goal line and works to maintain a proper view of play and the goalie. The home team is up by two goals, not quite the blowout at Liberty.

An attacking player passes to a teammate on my side of the ice. He receives the puck, skates towards the net, and lines up for a shot. I stand a few strides behind him when he launches the puck on net.

The drawn out duration of this shot reminds me of Rinaldi's game-winning comeback in high school. Time becomes more than relative as the puck flirts with my attention and leisurely strolls past opposing players. It hops over two sticks and challenges the goalie to a duel in the crease. Des remains composed, standing firm by the net with his back arched and whistle hand at the ready.

The puck entices the goalie to flinch prematurely and opens up a realm of potential entry points near the goal post closest to Des. The keeper sprawls outward to block the shot but completely misjudges its trajectory. Des creeps forward to maintain the best possible view of what now seems like an inevitable goal. Rink 3 grows impatient as parents, coaches, and players obsess over this lazy piece of rubber. It jaunts into the goal crease, takes one look around at its audience, and flings itself into the back of the net. The puck makes a firm indentation on the dirty interior padding and puffs up the meshing with a final flex of its muscles.

I wait for Des' goal point and a tweet from his whistle, the definitive recognition of this undoubtedly legal goal.

They never come.

Both arms rest at waist level while he still leans down at the goal. I stare at my brother as the seconds painfully drag beyond the puck's dance across the goal line.

What is he waiting for? C'mon Des!

I raise my whistle arm and contemplate blowing the play dead myself.

The puck entered the net, I saw it.

My whistle hand is just below chest level when Des backs off the goal crease and turns his attention to some faint shadow behind the net. The players show similar interest in this trick of the light and lunge after it.

Am I crazy, or are they chasing a phantom?

Des moves into the corner when players converge on this optical illusion. I rub my eyes and glide into the zone.

That shadow is no joke: it's a tuna-can sized piece of black rubber.

My stomach churns in coordination with the look of nausea across my brother's face. Play continues while strange murmurs begin oozing out of the stands and benches. My skates become off-balanced and crooked, like some magician's spell just dulled both blades. This new puck, or old puck, maybe the same puck, eventually exits the zone. I regain my focus, increasingly disturbed by this sequence of events, and blow play dead for a legitimate off-sides.

Des immediately skates over. "Did, did you see that?"

Confusion stalks us both. We turn away from the benches to prevent any coach or player from listening in on our conversation. Rink 3 teeters at the center of a seesaw and it's time to put an end to this madness.

"Des, I saw that puck enter the goal. I followed it all the way from the original shot."

He looks back at the net.

"I saw it go in too and was getting ready to call the goal but the puck appeared outside behind the net. I don't know how, and the players just started after it."

"Huh," I mutter. "I never had this happen before."

"Maybe we should go check the bottom of the net, see if there's a hole or something."

Des' instincts are those of a veteran. I follow him back into the zone and direct the goalie to the corner. We both lean down on one knee and investigate this peculiar crime scene, our role as referees now like a pair of detectives from Dick Wolf's famous *Law and Order* television series. We're not professional investigators, but what the hell, the least we can do is look.

I grab frayed laces on the back of the net and search for anything suspicious that may have allowed the puck to slip out behind the goal. We examine from left to right and nothing looks out of place. Then, like detectives discovering some clue before a commercial break, it all begins to make sense. We dig near the left post and pull where the laces attach to the metal frame. A hole the size of my closed fist appears after a few yanks.

"Take a look at this!"

Des points at the netting and turns his head towards me.

My inspection concludes the obvious. "Yeah," I sigh, "I think a puck could definitely pass through there."

We stand back up, back out of the goal crease, and skate behind the net. An animated group of parents bangs the glass behind us, making gestures and pointing wildly down at the goal. Their opinions are of no relevance to our official determination but nonetheless suggestive that something unique *might* have occurred.

The opposite side of that same area reveals a similar hole. Officials are required to complete net checks before every game and we did our duties before starting this one. It's weird to think we might've missed a laceration, but this hole was not apparent until after the lacing was forcefully tugged from the inside. Who knows, a stick or skate could have opened it during the game.

Rink 3 grows restless as parents, coaches, and players stand impatiently and demand conclusion to this unusual delay. One of the golden rules for stoppages is "the shorter the better," and we're definitely running on the longer side.

"Alright Des, what are you thinking?"

He grabs his fingers and responds after a few seconds' pause.

"We both saw a legal goal and I am 99.99 percent certain the puck popped out through the back of the net. I don't know how it happened, but this hole is a pretty good bet. What should we do?"

I look at him with a hand over my mouth to conceal my expression from the rest of the building.

"We both saw the puck enter, found a hole near its entry point, and you recall seeing it come out behind the net. What do *you* think we should do?"

Des' eyes beam with eagerness and excitement.

"Well, I guess we have a good goal."

That a boy! I smile. *Now we're talkin'.*

"How are we gonna tell everybody though?"

He hesitates, still new to the occasionally dramatic nature of our job. I must admit that I, when given the proper situation, can't help being a little animated with my officiating. Maybe it's the musician in me.

I lean closer to my brother. "Okay Des, now watch this."

There was only one way to conclude the matter. I lift my right arm, bend it at the elbow with extra flare, and then point with all sincerity at the net. I hold my pose for at least five seconds. Parents behind the glass cheer ecstatically while observers in the stands call for foul play, terrible officiating, and the like.

Des smiles from ear to ear.

"Now you've done it," he laughs, struggling to deny it was a pretty sound conclusion to this case. "Guess we need to explain everything to the coaches."

I motion him forward in the long trek to both benches.

"Let's see what we can do."

***

I try reengaging with our conversation at the bar, for the roasts are only improving in the small hours of the morning. Riley, like Rinaldi, is never one to miss a good chirp.

"Brocky, first you joke about my Bud, and now you're not even done your first beer. You telling me you're only going for one tonight? Unbelievable."

"Nah, nah, settle down, when the waiter comes back I'll ask for another."

I feign commitment to this new promise with a big gulp of my drink.

"You're on your way to six beers, right Brock?" chirps Delfin, evidently feeling fine from whatever he's drinking by now.

"We'll see Mike, can't rush these things."

I finish my first beer when the bartender arrives with another.

"Ah damn, I'm really feeling some of that good lookin' mac and cheese," announces Riley while licking his lips and eyeing up the food menu.

I leave him and Delfin to dream of warm, cheesy goodness and stare into my full glass with nothing more than my own unfinished recollections.

***

Des and I enter the official's room after the game's conclusion. We take off our helmets and sit down on pairs of wooden benches. The game ended without any other incidents and Des secured his first trip back to officiating with quite a story to tell.

"How do you feel about our big challenge today?" I ask, hoping that, despite our strange experience, he had an enjoyable time on the ice with his big brother.

Des looks up after unzipping his sweater. "That goal was a weird situation, but I enjoyed working through it with you and seeing your dramatic call."

"Agreed," I reply, now taking off my elbow guards. "I'm glad we had this experience together, was definitely easier to handle than with a complete stranger."

He nods his head. "It was cool to make an important decision like that, helped me improve my confidence on the ice."

"I could've been less dramatic with it," I admit, "but that's one thing to keep us engaged in the game. We work together, get the job done, and have a little fun along the way."

"Hopefully I'll get some more games in soon, I enjoyed myself. Plus, I got to see you look stupid out there."

I grin. "Ya, don't worry, you looked stupid too."

We officiated most of Des' games that season as a pair, picking up sets during tournaments to continue improving our abilities as two brothers wearing the same color stripes. I couldn't imagine a better way to "work" with my brother than getting out on the ice, making important decisions, and learning from each other. This particular game was a unique piece of our officiating scrapbook, one of many assignments where our relationship grew stronger with each and every icing call, penalty, coach conversation, and tough situation.

Sport is a fickle thing. While hockey rips people apart through line brawls at Liberty and season-ending fights with Rinaldi, it can also strengthen the closest bonds between friends and family. Whether I encounter hockey's most violent or benevolent tendencies cannot be said until that first step onto the ice.

The only aspect of Murph's doctrine I had yet to experience at Liberty was that officiating is an *art*, not a science. Though our trip down south was already halfway over when we left the bar, I had little doubt that Murph's first rule from

Harvard would prove itself in due time. Part two of the D1 Men's weekend schedule awaited us in under twenty-four hours, and if my second game was to be anything like the first, then I was beyond confident there'd be more than enough drama during my return to LaHaye Ice Center.

CONDUCTOR

How's music school treatin' ya kid? Have you ever thought about clarinet performance? Yo bro, what's good with your jazz studies? What's the deal with music education programs?

Hey, you went into music...right?

No. I did not study music. I love the arts but did not pursue them professionally.

There was a time when I might have made my own leap of faith on music as a career. In addition to PMEA concert bands, I also participated in three PMEA orchestra festivals. At the 2016 PMEA Region 6 Orchestra, my last event before All-States with Kitelinger, I played with the most talented high school students and orchestral musicians I ever met. I fondly recall the sweet sounds of woodwinds dancing a cloud layer above our ensemble in *Morning Mood* from Grieg's *Peer Gynt Suite No. 1* before the strings and heavy brass pounded away at Tchaikovsky's *Symphony No. 4* and furnished walls of symphonic steel in the grandiose finale to another PMEA festival.

Our conductor, interested in facilitating the next generation of musical leaders, asked a rather unique question during one rehearsal. She leaned forward on the podium and clearly enunciated every word to the entire group.

"Does anyone want to try conducting?"

A fervor arose among the musicians. Does she really mean it? I never saw the baton offered to a mere festival performer. I sat up and launched my right arm into the air like a referee witnessing the most obvious penalty.

Me, I yearned, *pick me!*

The first student received his opportunity, then the second got hers. I raised my arm each time to the eventual selection of another, but this was of no alarm, for the next one would be mine.

Our conductor retook her baton with my arm still raised.

"Alright, that's enough for now, time to break for lunch."

I persisted, nonetheless.

"Excuse me," I inquired, "is it possible I could try conducting after the break?"

"Sure," she replied, "we'll resume later."

We never did.

I used to wonder if my failure to conduct, and the decision not to major in music, were choices I would look back on with displeasure. Could conducting at Region Orchestra have entirely altered my life plans? Was this PMEA opportunity my last shot at the podium? Did I waste my potential? I can still imagine the rush of standing in front of that talented group, picking up the baton, and saying *yes*, I want to be a conductor.

I'll never know what would have happened if I had gotten my opportunity to conduct. That chance for a turning point toward music is lost to time, nothing more than a distant memory. Of the many questions I asked myself in the few years after my PMEA experiences, there was always one which left me guessing: *will I live with regret?*

On the one hand, I kept music in my life through involvement with PMEA, performances at Temple, and study of Irish music in Derry. Then again, some of my most decorated musical experiences like Balmages' rainfall performance and my first chair solo were one-time occurrences with no immediate pathway to other opportunities. Whether I had the potential to succeed as a musical conductor is a question I'll live with for the rest of my life. However, when I look back on my second game at Liberty, I believe our mysterious universe may have put me on the path of a conductor after all.

***

A cloud of frozen snow launches into the air and grazes my referee sweater. It sends chills down my body and draws out goosebumps underneath my equipment. I move backward along the boards, letting players pass in front of me. Sweat cascades off my brow and clings to the bottom of my visor, partially obscuring my view as I pursue play out of the defensive zone.

Delfin, Riley and I are back for round two with the D1 Men's. LaHaye Ice Center is packed once again from wall to wall with fans dressed in all shades of red, white, and blue. An old rival from the Eastern States Collegiate Hockey League, Liberty's D1 ACHA conference, is back in town.

Time stops after Liberty's goaltender freezes the puck. I skate to center ice and look at the scorekeeper, waiting for another TV timeout to expire. After a few moments of peace and quiet in an otherwise boisterous game, I receive a sign from the scorekeeper and begin the mechanics for restarting play.

The line change procedure is an often overlooked part of officiating duties. Linesmen and referees work together to ensure a smooth transition during stoppages, granting each team a fair and efficient substitution. The home team is always entitled to last change, though they have the right to forfeit that privilege. Successful officials use the line change procedure to build relationships with coaches and sometimes chat with players.

I turn to the visiting bench and point, making eye contact with their coach as he finishes changing all five skaters. My right arm springs up at the end of their final substitution. I then look over to Liberty's bench, point with my left arm, and mouth "You good?" to the head coach. He nods after glancing down at his notes and signals for both bench doors to close. I acknowledge his response and turn to the score-keeper with my right arm still raised. Delfin and Riley are directing players toward a faceoff in Liberty's defensive zone when the commercial light finally goes dark.

I get a thumbs-up from the scorekeeper and take a few crisp strides toward Riley. I drop my right arm to shoulder height, bend the elbow as to bring my forearm across my chest, and then point to Riley with the entire arm and all five fingers. Our eyes meet and he subsequently blasts his whistle. I leave my right arm extended for a few seconds and then drop it to my side before transitioning into ready position with my back tilted and hands on my knees. Riley squares both centers and drops the puck.

Liberty wins the draw and gains possession behind their net. They start breaking out of their zone and I respond with hard backward strides into the jagged ice, feeling the grooves and cracks vibrate along with those from an assortment of powerful college skaters. Liberty's breakout is successful and

I quicken my pace, first skating past center ice and then into the opponent's defensive zone. An icy wind cushions my back as I avoid contact with the Liberty rush and maintain a wide perspective of the incoming play.

The puck moves into the far corner and I inch along the goal line to optimize my line of sight. I can hear the crowd blasting horns and cowbells as one Liberty forward maneuvers out of the corner with possession of the puck and scans the ice for his teammates. Unable to find any passing lanes, he springs forward toward the opponent's goal crease with one lone defender in pursuit. The opponent catches up to him and their sticks collide, sending the puck up into the air. It rises just above the crossbar as both players begin falling to the ice. The Liberty forward lurches one hand into the air, reaches out for that black piece of rubber, and swats it with the combined momentum of their collision.

The opposing goalie springs upward but fails to block the puck. I watch it fly toward the top left corner of the net as both players and goalie land on the ice. The Liberty forward lifts his head and we both watch the puck dip just under the red crossbar and make a comfortable home in the back of the goal.

The gravity of this situation weighs like the sky on Atlas' shoulders. All building lights focus in on the net while over ten thousand eyes lock onto my position. I shudder under the intense stare of all skaters, bench players, coaches, staff, sportscasters, mascots, moms, dads, guys chirping me behind the boards, people watching on TV, and my three partners. They stand motionless and await my decision.

Refereeing is reactive, and as the puck steadies itself behind the goal line, I concern myself with one fact only: a hand propelled it into the net.

The time is right for quoting one of my favorite summer readings, recalling those laws and statutes that govern ice hockey. The ACHA uses the NCAA rule book and I reference the *2018-2019* and *2019-2020 NCAA Men's and Women's Ice Hockey Rules and Interpretations* as follows:

Rule 83.6 **Disallowed Goals** *– An apparent goal shall not be allowed by the Referee in any of the following cases:*
- *If an attacking player throws, bats or propels the puck into the goal with any part of the body.*

The rule book is my sword and shield. I will use it as such.

"NO!! NOOO!!" I bellow, bringing both hands together in front of my chest, elbows bent at ninety degrees. I scream again while thrusting my arms out to the side, elbows fully extended, fingers wide apart, palms normal to the ground. The building is suddenly silent, stunned by this lone referee.

I pull my arms in and wave again, this time raising them slightly higher than the first washout. I glide to the opposite corner and open up my body to face center ice. My arms still point outward as I gaze to both benches for a few seconds and allow my verdict to sink into the fabric of LaHaye. I drop my left arm and then extend my right arm in front of my body while forming a fist.

Neither bench erupts into protest, none of the players skate up in frustration or disbelief. Even the fans stay calm after the denial of another goal for their beloved Liberty Flames. Delfin meets my gaze with a nod and I take a few collected strides toward center ice. We then look at the linesmen. They return placid expressions in silent agreement with my no-goal decision.

I position myself at the edge of the referee's crease and face the scorekeeper. She looks up with a wide-eyed expression, clutching a pen and leaning over the scoresheet.

"No goal due to hand pass!" I decree, swinging my right arm forward with another clenched fist. The scorekeeper nods her head several times and scribbles a note onto the scoresheet.

I visit both benches to briefly explain my decision. The opposing team naturally shows no objection and I greet one of Liberty's coaches after arriving at their bench.

"Batted into the net with his hand, no goal."

"Okay, no problem," he responds, turning away toward his offense. I make eye contact with that same Liberty forward and return a look of silent understanding before leaving the bench.

My partners begin organizing the next faceoff as I retake that familiar position near center ice. No change from the opponent? Arm goes up, the other points at Liberty. Only two changes? No problem. Arm goes down, points, and rests by my side. I take the ready position, preparing for the uncertainty of the next play, when I suddenly begin to chuckle.

Damn, I think to myself. *I really am a conductor.*

***

Music and ice hockey. Most would require little observation to conclude they are completely different. Music is art, hockey a sport. It should be that simple, right?

Wrong. The perceived differences between these two activities are actually superficial. At their most fundamental level, music and hockey are about *people*. Musicians and hockey players work hard at a common goal with teammates, engage with other organizations, players, groups, officials, performers, conductors, composers, and everyone else that strives to better their respective communities.

Murph was right: officiating is an art form that thrives on relationships. I work those line changes at Liberty like a maestro, controlling time and the flow of play with every decision. My arm is a baton and the ice my podium. We officials are artists, regardless of league or level. My brother and I could be breaking up fights in Lynchburg or picking up pucks in Aston for all I care; in the end, we paint each game as a portrait of the individuals involved.

Relationships have already played crucial roles in every chapter of my life. Hockey brought me together with characters such as Rinaldi, Des, and Delfin, forming a family on the ice in more ways than one. The arts introduced me to others like Luke, Nathan, and Balmages who were all extremely influential in shaping my experiences with music. Maybe I never conducted at Region Orchestra or pursued music after some potential for an artistic career. Rather than lamenting the past and cursing all creation till the end of time, I find satisfaction in considering where officiating has taken me.

I began refereeing as a kid looking for cash. Six seasons later, I'm conducting on icy stages all across the country. I walked a tightrope between sport and art and secured a compromise to satisfy both of my passions. My personal contacts between hockey and music may not have known as much, but their combined efforts ultimately guided me to a new passion called officiating that filled what seemed like a musical void in my life. Though my days as a clarinetist and active referee will eventually come to an end, my social and professional connections within the music and hockey communities will prevent me, as I once feared after Region Orchestra, from living with regret.

As such, I present my fourth tool for navigating change: relationships.

Cultivating relationships while navigating multiple passions is no simple challenge, and I pose the following questions to accompany you in such a task:

What brought you to your current interests and relationships?

What similarities exist between your passions?

Which relationships led to and maintain your interests?

What threads your relationships together and tightens the knots between different aspects of your life?

The most intriguing questions are perhaps the following:

Are there deeper connections between your relationships and passions than you first thought? Might they open the door to new experiences and opportunities?

I hold no key to this series of intricate locks, no magic bean that will sprout some convenient vine between different elements and people in your life. It's quite possible that they're separated for good reason. Nevertheless, I ask that you examine your relationships and passions, for they might just help you realize, as I did, that you alone hold the power to forge connections between the seemingly disconnected.

After finally fusing my interests for music, ice hockey, and officiating in Fall 2018, I turned my attention back to my studies at Temple. *Building Bridges* and refereeing were integral parts of my college experience, but as I drive home with Delfin after our weekend at Liberty, questions regarding my major and post-collegiate plans come front and center once again. Though relationships have taken me far from the chaos of freshman year, they alone cannot decide what I'll do after college. I set myself on a unique course from physics to Derry, from Harvard to Liberty, and return to campus with little clarity regarding the next link in the chain. While I've navigated change with passion, dissent, holistic international education, and relationships, I do not have a solid response to Delfin's casual inquiries about my future.

There is but one question I am more than ready to answer. It's possible I'll receive it tomorrow, another repetition of "how's life in music school?" from an old, assuming friend. Maybe my response is once again no. I'm not studying music, not technically anyway. But, am I a part-time conductor?

I'll leave that one for you to decide.

SHIFTING DIRECTION

JACK OF ALL TRADES

Mechanical Engineering. There, I said it. It's the answer you've been waiting for and perhaps never expected.

I close my computer and set it down with a sigh. I look through the window to my right and spot the Schuylkill River during what must be my thousandth trip on the regional train to Temple University. It flows peacefully under the early morning sun and distances my mind from similar feelings of confusion you may be experiencing in this very moment.

Mechanical Engineering...what?

I promised an eventual discussion of my major after *Building Bridges* and the time has finally come to make sense of my studies.

I officially changed my academic program after returning from Derry. Physics was sidelined long before the onset of *Building Bridges*, and I had hoped study abroad would help me clarify which new major was right for me. Derry certainly refined my passion for holistic international education, but also had the ironic quality of pushing me toward an undergraduate program that hardly resonated with music, dissent, foreign culture, etc.

As I began my third semester and first term as a commuter in Fall 2017, I must admit that I still had dreams of teaching physics after a summer of anything but science. I left high school with the resolve to teach, and despite my love for *Dissent in America* and *Building Bridges*, I did not have the heart to completely diverge from my original goal of becoming a science educator. Like my passions for music and hockey, I did not see myself using dissent and international studies as the only means to build my future career.

People ask me to this day why I studied engineering, and I still question if it was wise to sideline passions in the pursuit of some separate profession. For better or worse, my thought process in late 2017 went back to the theme between Luke and Rinaldi. Both had their passions and found different means to incorporate them in the lives they wanted for themselves. The choice to study mechanical engineering, the most general of the engineering disciplines, was my own compromise between teaching, interests outside of school, and the influences from freshman year.

The switch to engineering was also an act of dissent against my original plans after high school. It did not completely remove me from the realm of science and technology but seemed to offer different pathways to teaching and industrial jobs. I had teachers in high school and at Temple who studied engineering and then made careers as educators. Both my parents studied mechanical engineering, and while my dad currently works as an engineer, my mom made a professional change to yoga and exercise fitness and never looked back.

Their stories, in combination with my own desire to balance my studies with music and officiating, gave me the impression that an engineering degree would provide a "jack of all trades" experience. I could complete standard engineering coursework, enjoy music and officiating in my free time, and eventually leave school with a versatile degree that could lead me to industry or, along with further education, help me find a teaching position.

The formula for my choice looked something like the following:

Hockey + Music + Physics + Dissent
+ Derry + Officiating
≈ Mechanical Engineering

There may be no similar equation offered in any engineering curriculum, no formula ever presented in a history textbook or on any piece of music. It was nevertheless the equation of my sophomore and junior years of college.

I would be naive to assert this choice was not without its drawbacks. Completing an engineering degree was no simple task, especially when my true passions were outside the realm of design projects, machine construction, and coding. Mechanical engineering quickly revealed itself to be a business degree among the sciences and fostered a significantly different atmosphere from classes like *Dissent in America* and *Building Bridges*.

For all the challenges brought on by engineering, there was one idea which helped me keep my resolve. My parents have always encouraged me and my brother to maintain positive attitudes, and I find their guidance best justified by Charles Swindoll's belief that "90 percent" of life is how we react to the uncontrollable situations, or the other "10 percent" of life, which we encounter. (Insight, 2021)

I first encountered Swindoll's idea in an auto repair shop waiting room and have kept it in mind ever since. We, and no one else, control our actions. Even in times of great strife, we retain that all-important choice of *how* to respond to any situation. Attitude keeps our emotions in check and is a powerful tool for planning the future we desire.

With Swindoll's belief in mind, I'll tip my hand early and decree my fifth ingredient for navigating change in young adulthood: attitude.

Attitude, like relationships, had its own role to play in my adolescence. Each and every choice made by myself or another person in my life depended on the attitude with which we approached a situation. Think back to Nathan Snyder and my first PMEA blunder: it was his attitude that helped me overcome failure and nail my second audition.

Refereeing further exemplifies the meaning of Swindoll's quote. It is a reactive art form, a craft which demands that officials, no matter what 10 percent they receive, rise to the occasion with a 90 percent response and serve the game of ice hockey. A fight, puck through the net, even an illegal goal; officials train themselves to respond appropriately in these situations, and the same can and should be said about our approach to life itself.

As I continue my train ride to Temple in mid-October 2018 with the Liberty weekend now behind me, I find my own philosophy on attitude being put to the test. My flexible combination of engineering, music, and officiating has come to an inflection point. The further I move along in my college curriculum, the more uncertainties I encounter.

This engineering compromise has been my jack of all trades, but it offers no specific prospect of where to go after college. I could teach, seek out opportunities in industry, enroll in graduate school, or pursue something completely different. Only one more undergraduate summer awaits me in 2019, a summer often described as crucial in one's professional development. I approach it at light speed, and while my colleagues arrange internships, apply for study abroad opportunities, and prepare for that "next step" in their lives, I stare out at the Schuylkill with no plan whatsoever. My engineering degree is here to stay, that 10 percent is certain. What I make of this unique sandwich between passions and major, the 90 percent response to my current predicament, might just be the most important decision I'll make in junior year. Life is pressing those important questions about what I want and how much I'm willing to fight for it.

After all this talk of bridges and engineering, Ralph Young once joked I could pursue civil engineering after college. He may have guessed the wrong profession, but Ralph was right about the construction business. Fall 2018 began many new bridges in young adulthood, and while some carried me far beyond my comfort zone, the first connected my return from Liberty with an all too familiar destination: *Dissent in America*.

ROGER WILLIAMS

The leather jacket is a crucial piece in every wardrobe. Built for almost any occasion, it offers the perfect balance of finesse and bristle, conformity and rebellion.

Leather jackets unite the generations in a single article of clothing. Running my hand along their smooth, weathered exterior conjures images of my grandfathers' high school outfits during the 1950's. They might as well have been characters out of Randal Kleiser's *Grease* with gelled hair, white T-shirts, and an attitude to match.

I stroll into the adjunct's office on the eighth floor of Gladfelter Hall with my leather jacket on full display. It's accompanied by sturdy brown boots, aged blue jeans, and none other than the classic white T-shirt. I doubt my friends would say I'm known for my style, but I'm at the peak of my game when the leather jacket comes out.

This is by no means my first visit to room 856. Aside from daily trips with the train, my most common commute within Temple's campus in this fall semester is to my lair among old computers and assorted history books. I enter the four-digit door code and place my backpack down on the most comfortable chair. Then comes my computer, lunch bag, and a binder labeled "Dissent."

It's been over a year since Ralph and I trekked Slieve League and I'm thrilled to be back in the classroom together, albeit in a different role than before.

Temple offers an undergraduate enrichment experience called the "Diamond Peer Teachers Program," a teacher-training internship where undergraduates partner with professors and act as an additional resource for students in undergraduate courses. Peer teachers attend lectures, organize weekly meetings for individual and group study, and facilitate student experiences. (Temple University, 2019)

I stayed in contact with Ralph well beyond our time in Derry, and while engineering may have been my primary focus at Temple, it didn't prevent me from securing a peer teaching position for *Dissent in America*. This was not my only instructional experience in college, as I worked as an undergraduate teaching assistant for engineering classes and labs during my final three years at Temple. However, despite its one-semester duration, my work alongside Ralph was easily the most formative of all my instructional opportunities as an undergraduate.

I embarked on another journey through *Dissent in America* with the holistic and international lenses I acquired in Derry. Our course material was no different than before, but my understanding of that term "American" changed after I took to the streets of Philadelphia, studied Irish culture in Derry, and attended Murph's Harvard camp.

Learning from Ralph is both inspiring and insightful into the world of collegiate-level instruction. I had been working with him for close to two months before my return from Liberty, collaborating on anything from organizational tasks to exam preparation. Although I have no complaints about the work itself as I hang up my leather jacket on this chilly day in late October 2018, there is one pressing item on my mind.

I have only one wish: more students.

Initial interest in my study sessions at the beginning of the semester fizzled out as the weeks went on. My daily commute back and forth from room 856 went from a communal process to an individual hobby. Each passing week in October made me worry it was something I did, or rather something I could not do, which accounted for the lack of student engagement. Though the true cause(s) of my empty study sessions may forever elude me, today was meant to be different.

I peek up at a knock on the office door and greet one lonely student waiting in the hallway.

"Hey, how's it going? What can I help you with today?"

Okay, I think, *maybe now's the chance for reviving my confidence and these study sessions.*

He sits down shyly in my office and pulls out his copy of *Dissent in America: The Voices that Shaped a Nation.* While it was Ralph's *Dissent: The History of an American Idea* that kept me company in the Johnny Ring Terrace, students in *Dissent in America* also read selections from his other major publication, *Dissent in America: The Voices that Shaped a Nation. Voices* is unique among the texts I read in college, for it is Ralph's compilation of important essays, speeches, songs, and other documents from American protesters. It is an encyclopedia of American dissent in the words of those who did it best.

My student flips through a few pages of *Voices* before arriving at a bookmark on Roger Williams and *The Bloudy Tenent of Persecution.* Williams was an English colonist who, like many others, made the risky journey from Europe to a world that was still very much new in the 17th century. Ralph also notes how Williams is known for founding the colony of Providence in Rhode Island in 1636. (Young, 2009)

The thought of his English ancestry brings me back to the British Isles, and then Northern Ireland, Derry, Sean, Gudrun, the hikes, the protests; I'm sucked out of room 856 and thrown into Sandinos, licking my lips after creamy sips from a freshly poured pint of Guinness while traditional Irish melodies dance on the counter in front of me and an image of some revolutionary on the wall triggers an avalanche of thoughts about the Troubles and my place in the world.

Oh Derry. How I miss you so.

It takes a few blinks to bring me back into Gladfelter.

"Ah yes, the Roger Williams. What would you like to do with it today?"

He looks down at the table.

"I need to study for the midterm next week but didn't know where to start. I still don't get most of the text."

"Have you reread through it at all?"

"Nope." His shoulders shag.

Perfect, I think to myself, *I'm out of practice with this teaching business, my first student is completely stumped, and Derry bounces like a pinball inside my head.*

"Well, gotta start somewhere," I grumble, forcefully sliding my computer to the end of the table. I cough, move my chair, and peer up at the ceiling before down at my student.

"You sure we can read it today?" He hesitates like a soldier whose pride overshadows his wounds.

I look over to him and our eyes meet. My mind races in the split second between his last statement and my necessary response. Both hands begin to sweat and I readjust myself in my seat.

Negativity is a strong but by no means overpowering emotion. Although it's been a discouraging few weeks, the least I can do is try and help the one student who bothered to visit my office. I take a deep breath, clear my mind, and focus on attitude. Just 10 percent of this situation comes from our collective preparation and the other 90 percent depends on our response. This study session might not be my best work, but I owe this student my full effort.

I reset my shoulders, sit up in the chair, throw on a smile. A positive attitude isn't among my possible responses: it's the only one.

"Yep, no problem." I move my chair closer to his and put both hands on the desk. "Let's see what we can do."

I structure our analysis like a biology experiment. We dissect Williams' points line by line and split apart individual sentences to extract their DNA. He writes in a typical style for something published in 1644, both elegant and complex. Williams constructs *Tenent* as a conversation between opposing viewpoints, adding another level of difficulty to deciphering his commentary on religious and political statutes in British colonial government. He is credited for proposing ideas similar to the separation of church and state in his *Tenent*, that religion and government should do nothing more than coexist. (Young, 2009) Although this notion was a constant theme in my public school education, I never learned of Roger Williams until studying with Ralph in 2016.

It is bitter work, fighting through lines of analogy so thick and dense that we struggle together as teacher and student on a voyage to Colonial New England. We travel without fear of what lies ahead, yanking the ropes and tending to the sails on our ship through the early transatlantic storm called *Tenent*. Just when it seems we might fail to interpret Williams' writing, properly prepare for the upcoming midterm, and survive this maelstrom of colonial literature, we recheck our course and continue sailing forward.

I pose the most important question after we finish the final paragraph.

"What seems to be Williams' main point?"

"Hmm," contemplates the student. "I'd say something about the separation of church and state?"

"Yeah, I'd have to agree."

"That's great, but, hold on. Wait a second."

He lifts his head up from the book with a bright light in his eyes.

"Don't we still struggle with exactly defining this idea?" He flips through a few pages and pulls out his notebook.

"I feel like I see news about people arguing over this in school."

"Absolutely," I reply. "Think about schools trying to have the Bible in class or teach Creationism. This text is pretty old, but I'd say it's still really important today."

"That's incredible!" he exclaims. "I can't, I can't believe this idea of separation was introduced so long ago."

I lean back in my chair and smile. "Some people take it for granted and forget this idea came from dissenters like Williams."

"Yeah, really. And Dr. Young said we'll be talking about other important dissent that still impacts our daily lives? Things we haven't figured out completely?"

"You know it. We have to keep reaching for our founding ideals, even if they're almost three hundred years old."

He scribbles a few notes before putting away his notebook and copy of *Voices*. "Man, I'm glad I came in today. Thanks Adam."

I wish him good luck and he departs, leaving me alone once again with my leather jacket.

As the weeks went on, I began to analyze the role of attitude in my relationships with students and teachers. A positive approach to peer teaching led to enjoyable and productive study sessions, further improved my dynamic with Ralph, and brought me closer to the entire *Dissent in America* community. My attitude worked hand in hand with Murph's doctrine about building new relationships and convinced me of a single fact: I will always control my 90 percent response. The way I react, regardless of my 10 percent situation, is often more consequential than the obstacles I face.

My lessons with attitude impacted more than just the fall semester. When thinking of the coming summer and my post-collegiate plans, those thoughts of Derry began merging with my desire to teach and make good use of my 90 percent. Engineering was my 10 percent situation, and if my work with Roger Williams highlighted one thing besides the separation of church and state, then it was how attitude could change my reality. Though I had no idea what I was going to do with my passion for holistic, international, and relationship-based instruction, each and every study session in room 856 undoubtedly increased my resolve to *keep teaching*.

In fact, the Diamond Peer Teachers Program wasn't the only force guiding me toward education. My mechanical engineering coursework also supported my interest in teaching as the semester went on. It even helped me discover new opportunities after graduation, but only after making one simple demand.

I had to reach my breaking point.

THE NUMBERS

"Can anyone give me the answer to the first home-work problem?"

The student sitting to my left is met by nothing but silence on what is a frigid morning in early November 2018. I sit in an off-campus apartment, scribbling notes and staring down an intimidating set of engineering problems with my peers. I don't know a majority of the group but figured I could try and collaborate with them for the first time today. Thanksgiving break is only two weeks away, and though each passing minute brings me closer to the fall holiday, this impromptu study group succeeds in dragging out every minute for as long as humanly possible.

"Hey, can someone show me their numbers?"

Ah yes, the numbers, those light gray indents on my page. They pale in comparison to the memories I hold so dearly. Images of the Northern Irish coast drift through my consciousness, providing relief from what is another repetitive homework problem. Traditional Irish music from Sandinos fills my ears despite the ongoing silence between members of our study group. A swig from my metallic water bottle spills over my tongue like silky Guinness, the bread of beers, that which too often left the taps of Derry and found its way into my pint glass. The Troubles, several hikes, our holistic education; they splash all over my binder.

"Hey guys," I announce, "I'm gonna take a break outside. Back in a few."

I throw on my leather jacket, step outside the apartment building, and plug in my earphones. A few minutes' rest offers just enough time for some relaxing tunes.

The music of dissenters like Pete Seeger shuffles to the top of my playlist, his criticism of Lyndon Baines Johnson and the Vietnam War highlighted in songs like *Waist Deep in the Big Muddy - Live*. I escape the present through my earphones and recollections of past protests like one at the University of Wisconsin in 1967. Wisconsin students were brutally beaten by police after protesting the university's involvement with the Dow Chemical Company, the primary manufacturer of Napalm during the Vietnam War. (Board of Regents, 2019) I wonder if any *Dissent in America* students will ask about this in my office hours tomorrow.

Damn, looks like I've already been outside for nearly half an hour. I reenter the apartment and another student tries leading the group.

"Okay, let's do this next problem together. Someone give me their numbers."

Ah yes, the numbers, those light gray indents on my page. This new problem falls flat to the rush of a chilly breeze under my visor on the ice at Liberty. My baton shoots into the air for an upcoming penalty assessment as the crowd rocks a boat named LaHaye. Five thousand fans deafen my ears during the Six for Six fight while the chair I'm currently sitting in hardly compares to the cushy passenger seat in Delfin's car. I sit silently and look around at my peers like I stared at my fellow musicians and audience members at the 2016 PMEA All-State Band concert. A smile runs across my face at the thought of playing with great friends like Luke Simons after two successful PMEA auditions. What I would give to be back on stage and the ice.

A sudden burst of chatter interrupts my daydreams into the past. Several students begin arguing over a variety of possible answers for one singular problem.

"Come on guys," shouts someone at the far side of the room, "we need to be careful with our numbers. They have to be right!"

I roll my eyes for what is not the first time today.

Numbers, it's always numbers.

I've encountered scenarios during my studies where the majority of my success on an engineering assignment was dictated by a final numerical result and not the process I used or the scientific thinking involved in my analysis. The old saying goes that bridge designs should be pass or fail; the bridge either stands or crumbles. I do not advocate for a world in which we judge structures by something other than their performance unless we're looking to repeat the infamous collapse of the Tacoma Narrows Bridge. However, I do wonder if modern engineering education too frequently uses numbers as the only measure of success in students' academic pursuits. With every numerical homework problem arrives that cyclical pattern of confidence, the pregnant pause when checking an answer key, and an eventual prayer of Lord, please, have mercy, just let me get it right *next time*. As if that bridge design really allows for another...

I abandoned a physics degree long ago because my situation demanded change. Despite my transition away from that major, I still seek an understanding of the natural world and greatly appreciate physicists because they are concerned with scientific analysis, calculation, and how their numbers describe the universe. Eric Scheidly taught me to love physics because it is indeed a language, the universal code for the world we inhabit. Spiritual and symbolic understanding of the universe from the quantum to macroscopic levels yields nothing less than the keys to unlocking reality.

There are certainly engineering courses which promote an understanding similar to Scheidly's. I fondly recall one class that challenged me and my peers with the fundamental notions of thermodynamics, the Maxwell Relations, phase changes, and the history of scientific discoveries. I left those lectures understanding how materials and their thermodynamic properties behave, a satisfaction that far surpassed any feelings of success after plug-and-chug calculations.

Although some mechanical engineering classes may bring me closer to an appreciation of the natural world, I feel quite far from Scheidly's inscription of *language* as I approach the start of 2019. The easy solution to my frustrations in this group study session would be to switch majors and take my idealistic understanding of the real world and run with it. Maybe I will cling to that understanding one day, though certainly not until after the conclusion of this degree.

Regardless of what *I* do, I posit that engineering education needs to better prepare students for engagement with the world as well-rounded individuals. Tomorrow's engineers cannot just be engineers; mankind is entering a period in history where science demands those wielding its power must understand the social, political, economic, and cultural repercussions of their work. In addition to pursuing numbers, students should be trained to question authority, engage in a globalized society, and understand their duties in the quest to improve sustainability and equity for all people.

Numbers have an undoubtedly critical role in fields from engineering to medicine. They lie behind the life-saving vaccines made by my dad and his colleagues at Merck, the renewable energy technology used to fight climate change, and the super-computing technologies of the future. My generation is beyond lucky to live in a time of rapid innovation and I remain forever grateful to those wielding numbers for the benefit of mankind. However, science and engineering curricula should not be so hell-bent on pursuing numbers that students lack exposure to other subjects which promote critical thinking, develop communication skills, and study culture.

Now and then I'm asked why I venture outside of my engineering coursework and study topics like dissent and Irish history. Some of my peers cannot understand how general education courses about culture, philosophy, and the arts could matter to an engineering student. I pose them the following questions in rebuttal:

Is medical equipment sold for patients or dollar bills?

Should anyone design weapons without understanding their ethical use?

Why did Wisconsin students dissent against the production of Napalm?

Society cannot function without morals, and though a few extra humanities classes do not guarantee a well-rounded education, I suggest that increasing the number of liberal arts courses in engineering curricula would further improve engineers' conception of not only *what* to do in the real world but *why* and *for whom.*

Maybe my belief in balancing STEM education with the liberal arts is just for now, maybe I'm just an idealist in my twenties. Or, maybe it's by studying technical and non-technical subjects, obtaining the right mixture of scientific experiences, holistic investigation of our modern society, and opportunities for personal development, that engineers can best fulfill their scientific and moral obligations to our species and the Earth.

Let me be clear: engineers are a clever bunch and Temple produces many talented and qualified graduates every semester. I hold no grudge against my college or peers, but it's just that I'm tired, burnt-out from solving repetitive problems like a machine and stacking myself next to my colleagues on the conveyor belt of our careers.

I pursued physics and engineering because I wanted to teach and admired my former instructors in high school who fostered my interest in the sciences. As someone who may very well become a STEM educator in the future and simply cares about the impact of modern engineering, I acknowledge my discontentment with my current trajectory because I want to make a positive impact on engineering education. Having such an effect on curricula and instructional strategies requires analysis of both their strengths and areas where they could perhaps do better. I highly value the impact of engineering in society and see greater diversity of subject matter in engineering curricula as an efficient means of improving STEM education in the future.

Even after two years of engineering school, I still retain my drive to inspire the next generation but have no idea where my path will take me. I knew long ago that engineering would be independent of my passions, but I'm beginning to reconsider the balance between my true interests, career goals, and course of study. What I would give to go back to Europe as a student, let alone find a holistic teaching job either at home or overseas. What a life it would be to immerse myself in a truly different part of the world, one which would perhaps offer perspectives contrary to those I've experienced over the past two decades. Regardless of where I find myself next summer and after college, I am determined to shift away from my engineering studies and find a career driven by passion. I may not be going all-in on conducting or professional officiating, but the need to find a holistic teaching job, whether in STEM or some other discipline, is more urgent than ever before.

Sometimes the solutions to life's problems come in bits and pieces, spread out like breadcrumbs in a river that reunite downstream. Other times it's in moments of crisis, a breaking point, that seeds are planted for the future.

I leave the study group with my leather jacket in hand and begin a quick journey to campus. The coldness from earlier in the day has recently given way to sunlight and fresh air, and the gray clouds of my morning commute are now overwhelmed by radiating solar warmth. I arrive at Temple's Tuttleman Learning Center and take a single flight of stairs up to the second floor. As I make a left and begin the long, straight walk down the second-floor corridor, my eyes shift right to Temple University's Education Abroad Office, now closed for the day. I wander over to a collection of folders stapled to the wall. Each contains flyers for summer study abroad programs in every corner of the world.

Photos of the unknown trigger musings of Derry and provoke my nostalgia like the smell of any Sandinos' trough urinal haunts the nose. My fingers run over names like Prague, Athens, and Tokyo before stopping at one slightly crinkled flyer for Temple University's Intensive German language summer program in Leipzig, Germany. It reads as follows:

Take your language skills to the next level by partici- pating in Temple's Intensive German language program in

Leipzig. The four-week or eight-week program is designed for undergraduates who have completed at least one semester of university-level German, and is best suited for those who are looking for an immersive experience with opportunities for independent exploration of German culture.

I quickly scan the entire flyer and examine this real opportunity to study the German language in eastern Germany. (Temple University, 2018) Then I grab a second flyer, break away from the display, and disappear down the hallway.

A NONTRADITIONAL CANDIDATE

Typing resumes on my black computer keyboard. A digitized *Program Description* for Temple University's Leipzig summer program consumes the screen:

You will spend the first few days of the program in Berlin and then travel as a group to the Herder Institut of the University of Leipzig. Faculty from the Institut will teach you in a course that reflects your German language level, and you can expect to further your language skills through the group project component...your on-site program director, Dr. Patricia Melzer...will lead several excursions and activities within Leipzig...attending a Bach Music Festival concert, watching a soccer match on a screen in one of the main plazas, and taking in the magnificent architecture and historical monuments on a walk through the city are some favorite student activities in Leipzig.

Thoughts of language education elicit memories of Scheidly, Derry, and Dr. Barbara Gorka, the Director of Temple's Fellowships Advising Office. I burrow into my congested email inbox and fight through a traffic jam of course announcements until finding an email from Barbara. She mentions various research grants, attractive opportunities for graduate study, and post-undergraduate programs for teaching English abroad.

Those English teaching programs jump out of the screen. I fervently click from email to website, from student testimonial to promotional video. The name of a nationally funded fellowship program rests on the tip of my tongue.

Ah, Fulbright's the name.

I eventually find the website for the U.S. Fulbright Program, a fellowship sponsored by the Institute for International Education. The page for *140 English Teaching Assistant Awards* in Germany indicates that English teaching assistants work in German schools, collaborate with English teachers, and help educate their students about American society and the English language.

My mouse springs across the screen to a different tab and clicks on Fulbright Austria's website for US Teaching Assistantships at Austrian Secondary Schools. Their homepage *Live and teach English abroad in Austria* describes the nature of being an English teaching assistant, the benefits of working with Austrian students, and the value of representing the United States while learning about life in Austria.

I nod my head while further examining both English teaching assistantship programs and soak in the potential to represent my country overseas in Europe.

A notification for "low computer battery" flashes onto my screen. I wipe sweat from my fingers, close my computer lid, and dissolve into our front porch futon in mid-November 2018. Repetitive mouse clicks finally recede to the subtle whispers of diatonic wind chimes and birds on our Japanese Maple tree. A gentle breeze permeates the mesh window screens on our porch, seducing bits of steam from my coffee mug as I look out into our front yard.

Streaks of sunlight accompany memories from my childhood. I can hardly recall how many books I read, history shows I watched, and hours I spent learning about Germanic culture as a kid. My family and I muse over our ancestral legends every now and then, thinking back to the original Brocks who found their way to America from central and southern Europe. We even took a trip to Germany and Austria in June 2017 and traveled from the Black Forest to the home of Mozart before I flew to Derry for *Building Bridges*.

Those engineering numbers, truth be told, made me realize I needed to try something new at Temple. There was just one empty square left in the convoluted Sudoku puzzle of my undergraduate journey, and my recent trip to the study abroad office was the first of many steps in filling it. Nothing spikes my curiosity more than thoughts of studying German, returning to Europe, and then using my experiences to apply for English teaching fellowships in Germany and Austria. Studying in Leipzig would continue the holistic international education started in Derry, allow me to explore my other passions in a city with rich musical and athletic traditions, and then prepare me to build new relationships with Europeans as an American teaching English overseas.

I can hardly sit still at the thought of starting my career as an educator in Germany or Austria. What better way could there be to continue learning about international education, foreign ice hockey culture, and incredible music history, let alone qualify myself for future teaching positions, than to go abroad and teach American culture in Europe? There's only one "problem" with my plan, a question I often receive when mentioning my interest in something other than those numbers and working in the United States:

Adam, how can you possibly go teach in Europe when you know nothing about the German language and never taught English before?

I never studied German but excelled in Spanish classes during middle and high school. I never taught English before but tutored, worked as an undergraduate teaching assistant, and gain new experiences every day through peer teaching. I was never a cultural ambassador but bridge the divide between music and hockey, two popular activities in German-speaking countries, with my duties as an ice hockey referee.

There is a first time for everything, and as excitement rushes through my veins at the thought of returning to Europe through language learning, it seems that Leipzig and programs like Fulbright might just be the future I was looking for, the means to connect all the dots in my undergraduate journey.

Despite my attitude toward these opportunities, such a shift in my post-collegiate plans still requires the support from the people closest to me. I pause for a second, grab my phone, and then dial a familiar number as the sun reaches the highest point in its path on this Saturday afternoon.

Some people enter our lives as though they had been lurking in the shadows, waiting for a beam of light to reveal them as friends for life.

Ivy Chen is one such friend.

She is the Rinaldi of Temple, our relationship the product of having lived across from each other during freshman year without knowing until after I returned from *Building Bridges*. Ivy studies German and mechanical engineering, a convenient pair considering our mutual coursework and my interest in a language she already knows. While I was with Ralph in Derry, Ivy partook in the 2017 Leipzig program and has a close relationship with Dr. Patricia Melzer, the program director. We also happen to share a mutual interest in applying for fellowships after graduation. Ivy wants to conduct engineering research in Germany but is not yet ready to take a chance on Fulbright applications.

She answers my call with friendly banter before I transition to the most serious topic on hand.

"Oh right, Fulbright..." Her voice trails off into silence.

"Ivy, you're not feeling it anymore? I thought this was what you wanted."

"I don't know Adam," she sighs, "some of my professors suggest I shouldn't do Fulbright. They're advising me to pursue graduate school or industrial jobs instead."

I place my computer down to the side.

"They say *not to pursue it*? Why?"

"Melzer's been supportive," she notes, "but others say it's too competitive, my research background isn't good enough, and that I'm just not cut out for it. Part of me doesn't even want to take the risk, but then again, I don't know when else could we ever apply for these experiences."

"Agh!" she utters. "What have you been thinking?"

"Leipzig looks great and I'm liking these English teaching programs," I respond. "Suppose I'm in a similar spot. Haven't talked to anyone close about it and realize I'm no traditional candidate for English teaching."

"You're right," she jokes, "you are a nontraditional candidate."

We both get a laugh out of that one.

"That could help you stand out to Fulbright though," she continues, "same for me I suppose."

"We're both not stereotypical applicants," I remark. "But hey, I wasn't average for Derry and look where that brought me. As long as we do everything we can to get these grants, what's there to stop us besides ourselves?"

"A rejection might," Ivy chuckles.

"True," I fire back, "but if I really can learn German with Melzer and we both write strong applications, then I think we'll have a shot. The least we can do is try."

"Hmm," she says, "I guess it's about the attitude we go in with."

So it does come back to attitude. A 90 percent investment in learning German, studying in Leipzig next summer, and a well-written application could very well be enough to qualify me for fellowships and properly respond to my 10 percent situation.

"Ivy," I ask, "are we about to give in to everyone saying we can't do this shit when they themselves may have never tried?"

"Naw," she laughs back, "maybe not!"

We transition to other topics like any engineering drama and our next group trip to Chinatown before ending our call and moving on with the day. I place my phone down next to my computer, take another sip of my coffee, and look out once again into the front yard.

Fulbright is the opportunity to invest in ourselves and the future. While some of Ivy's contacts aren't ready to make a wager on her goals, and though I've hardly spoken to anyone in my inner circle about my German plans, no one on the outside can stop us from trying to win a Fulbright grant. I cannot understand the senseless doubters, all those chanting *No!* because our views do not align with their own reservations and fear of the unknown. Will Ivy and I really let insecure voices push us off the paths we want to travel and pull the rug out from under us because they think we can't stand on our own?

I reject their doubt, because in moments of conviction, there is perhaps no one better to believe in ourselves than ourselves.

That being said, I'll readily admit that a sprint to Leipzig and English teaching fellowships still seems somewhat rash after our pump-up phone call. I spent the last few years doing everything but German language learning, let alone English teaching. How could Fulbright make sense for me when it does not seem to align with the skill set and qualifications I amassed since high school?

Despite initial thoughts to the contrary, I realized my past did prepare me for something like English teaching in Germany or Austria. There are still many things I need to learn (like German) in order to study in Leipzig and win a Fulbright grant, but I am convinced the last few years, even if I didn't know as much, were bending my trajectory towards the German-speaking world. When thinking back to my relationships and history with ice hockey, music, dissent, Derry, officiating, engineering, and peer teaching, I sit on the porch with the belief that these experiences have set the stage for learning German. Studying in Leipzig and working as an English teacher will demand a well-rounded skill set and that's exactly what I've assembled over the last several years. Those skills, along with a positive attitude, might just be what I need to find the holistic teaching job I've been searching for all along.

I finally met with Barbara Gorka (as described in the Author's Note) in the week after my call with Ivy. Barbara supported my interest in Leipzig and teaching English abroad after graduation, and though my application would be no easy endeavor, it seemed the stars were aligning in my favor. The critical support from those like Ivy and Barbara was falling in line with my own convictions and propelling me towards a new chapter in my time at Temple. There were only two more individuals I needed to consult before fully committing to this German adventure: my parents.

TAKING A LEAP OF FAITH

I greatly respect the waning days of each year. The finale of our revolution around the sun yields a gentle transition from autumn to winter, from whispers of life to restful slumber. My mom is particularly fond of the "ber" months: Septem<u>ber</u>, Octo<u>ber</u>, Novem<u>ber</u>, Decem<u>ber</u>. These final chapters in the Earth's cyclical habit plant seeds for a promising future, one only encountered after the final page in every annual calendar.

While my parents and I prepare an outdoor fire on what is a crisp, clean day in late November 2018, I must admit there's more on my mind than the changing seasons. It's been almost a month since my discovery of Leipzig and Fulbright, registration deadlines for German I in Spring 2019 are drawing near, and I have not yet revealed my new German plan to my parents. English teaching in Europe seems to be the road least traveled for someone like myself who studies engineering, but with any luck, today will officially start my pursuit of English teaching fellowships. I seek my parents' support to quell any lingering doubts about my path forward, and while I know not what they'll say, I am certain of one thing.

Leipzig, for the moment, is about the only plan I've got.

My dad leans down to light our fire while my mom sits to his left in a black reclining chair. A chalice of cold European beer rests by her side as I angle my seat toward the firepit.

"So pal," she begins, "what exactly did you want to talk about?"

I take a sip of my drink and rest it on one knee.

"I want to start studying German. I've been doing a lot of thinking lately and found a way to study abroad in Germany this summer. After that, I could apply for English teaching assistantships in Germany and Austria after graduation."

Timid bursts of orange light sparsely color the pit as baby flames consume crunchy twigs and piles of autumn leaves. Let it be known: these crinkled travelers are fun to admire and serve more purposes than meets the eye!

My dad looks up from the pit and my mom takes another sip of her drink. They both raise their eyebrows in uniform fashion.

"Study German?" he questions.

"I found an opportunity to study abroad in eastern Germany over the summer and really want to do it. I'd need to take German I this spring and then apply for Temple's Leipzig program."

An occasional breeze twirls the fire and spreads it to all corners of the pit. Any feelings of warmth remain out of reach from my seat.

"I talked to Barbara, our fellowships adviser, and have been researching English teaching programs. I could use my language study in Germany, time in Northern Ireland, and all other experiences during the last few years to qualify for a position."

"What made you think of these programs specifically?" inquires my mom. "Our trip to Germany was great, but the idea of learning German is completely new to me."

Orange licks from the hungry flames taunt my concentration.

"I'm at a crossroad between engineering and education and want to take a chance on something different like German, to pursue an interest that could help me find a teaching position after graduation."

"But what exactly is the plan then?" asks my dad.

The flames begin consuming tiny logs as he sits down in his chair.

"Well," I start, "I didn't anticipate studying a foreign language at Temple, but engineering isn't cutting it right now and I think this German path will bring all my interests together. Going to Leipzig would be a fun addition to music and engineering and I know Ivy enjoyed her experiences there in 2017. I could then spend the rest of the summer writing applications for English teaching fellowships. Positions in Germany and Austria are difficult to get, but I believe I could make a competitive application."

"It seems you've been doing your research," notes my dad while shifting his chair slightly closer to the fire. "What kinds of candidates are those fellowships looking for?"

The heat begins to warm my outstretched legs.

"These programs want young graduates who are successful in their studies, well-rounded, and can speak to different aspects of American culture. I can represent engineering, music, ice hockey, studies of dissent, and my experiences in Derry."

The blaze grows stronger by the second. Cracks and pops from burning logs fade in and out of my explanations.

"I know I haven't taught English before, but after discussing it with Barbara, I think I could sell myself as a guy with enough interests to offer a unique view of the United States to my students. It also helps that I've been peer teaching for Ralph's class."

My mom nods while my dad adds more wood to the dancing flames.

"Yes," she responds, "it really does seem that you've been doing your research and thinking deeply about this. What's your plan for after these programs though?"

"Either graduate school or finding a teaching job somewhere. I know this was not my original plan, but I believe teaching overseas would help me apply for future programs and ultimately make me a better instructor. Plus, what a great experience before going back to school!"

Large flames begin cascading upward and spread to the edges of the pit as my dad turns back toward me.

"Are you prepared to accept the possibility that learning German alongside all other commitments may be quite difficult? And, even if you do go to Leipzig, that these programs may not accept you?"

I place my drink down on the ground after a cleansing breath.

"Yes, I am prepared. I know this will be an uphill battle and realize there are many steps to my current plan. However, I do believe this gamble is really worth the risk. I don't know another time in my life where I'll have the chance to at least try something like studying German and teaching English overseas."

They sit there quietly, beers in hand with neutral faces.

"At the end of the day, I look at this situation with a can-do attitude. I want to be content knowing that I gave it my all, even if I get rejected. I don't want to pass up this unique opportunity."

The silence across from me persists, interrupted only by cracks and pops from the fire. My parents remain plain-faced with their eyes focused on the flames. One, two, three seconds elapse as creeping voices of doubt, both internal and from all those chanting *No!* to Fulbright, wait to pounce on my only plan for the future.

My parents swirl their drinks and exchange glances. I lean forward in my chair when my mom turns back toward me.

"Adamnick," she begins with my childhood nickname, "I think this will certainly be a challenge for you, but when has that been a problem before? If you accept the terms of your situation and put your heart into it...then what else can we say but yes?"

"You seem so thrilled about this opportunity," interrupts my dad, "and I agree it would be amazing to go abroad this summer and then teach English. If shifting direction to German is what you really want and will work for, then it's the right path for you."

"Also," interjects my mom, "you have the right attitude about those fellowships if they don't work out. Look back at PMEA and freshman year. Things hardly go as planned, but when you have the right mindset, I think you'll make the best of your situation."

"In other words," she concludes, "barring no unforeseen surprises next semester, you have our support."

"Fantastic, thank you!!" I exclaim. "I'm in this to win it, and with the support of you all and my friends at school, who knows where this new adventure will take me."

The flames retreat back to the center of the pit at the sound of my parents' approval. We raise our glasses for a cheers as the fire burns contently in the background.

***

My mom likes to joke how she and my dad spent many days driving my brother and me all around the "tri-state area" for hockey and music. She's right, they really did. Through thick and thin, our parents have always been there for us.

Their backing of my German plan was still by no means guaranteed. It took a detailed rationale to convince my parents how a trip to Leipzig, let alone an English teaching position in Europe, were realistic possibilities for my future. While I theoretically could have pursued study abroad and fellowships without their support, I must admit I was not ready to make such a commitment without their input and the backing of others like Ivy and Barbara. I had great excitement and confidence about a new adventure overseas, but only overcame my own internal doubts about Leipzig and fellowships after speaking to my parents.

We all are powerful forces in our own right and should be our primary source of conviction and self-confidence; however, we must also remember that the support of family and friends, while not always necessary, is often invaluable when taking on life's greatest challenges.

I can recall many moments during my first two years at Temple when I knew not where I was going, hitched to an autumn leaf that was certainly taking me *somewhere*. This conversation with my parents is when that somewhere defined itself. My passions in high school and college are finally coming together as one and I plan to weave the yarn of my past into two new destinations: Leipzig and a German-speaking land thereafter.

After diverging from engineering and setting my sights on fellowships after Temple, I update the equation of my junior year as follows:

Hockey + Music + Physics + Dissent
+ Derry + Officiating
≠ Mechanical Engineering

I will thread the needle on this sewing project called German with one simple tool: attitude. It will help foster new experiences, motivate me to move forward despite any challenges, and manage my response to anything that doesn't go as planned. Attitude cannot guarantee I make the right decisions, but ensures I control every reaction to my successes and failures, accomplishments and letdowns.

While I may be unable to change the actions of yesterday, I still ask myself the following questions when preparing to take on tomorrow. Like before, I pose them similarly to you:

What is your current 10 percent situation?

What are your options for making the proper 90 percent response?

How will attitude prepare you for future actions and changes in perspective?

Whose support will you seek?

Never forget that every 90 percent response is yours and yours alone. You control how you react to the world and make a better future for yourself and the people you love. No 10 percent problem can ever take that ability from you.

Flash forward six months to May 2019 and my departure for Germany is but days away. While Chris Rinaldi used his 90 percent to start playing ice hockey in middle school, I'm using mine to head back to Europe. The time is ripe to embrace another turning point in my life, and I'm taking a leap of faith on Leipzig.

LEIPZIG, GERMANY

GOSENSCHENKE "OHNE BEDENKEN"

I don't believe there is anything in the whole earth that you can't learn in Berlin except the German language.
—Mark Twain

Mark Twain was a titan among writers. Prolific as both an author and humorist, he is one of the greatest names to ever line the American bookshelf. I must admit I have hardly scratched the surface of his literary contributions and stack his books, along with a great many others, in an ever-growing collection to read during the next few decades of my life.

Twain visited Germany multiple times during the 19th century and wrote about his experiences in *A Tramp Abroad, The Awful German Language,* and *A Tramp in Berlin.* Though the above quote from Andreas Austilat's revised version of *A Tramp in Berlin* may imply otherwise, Twain was also a student of the German language. He describes the nuances and sometimes confusing nature of learning German as an English speaker in *The Awful German Language,* exactly the type of material to motivate a young student like myself.

Twain may have never been to Leipzig, but his German musings are nevertheless on my mind as I board the regional train from Berlin to Leipzig in June 2019. My suitcase is fully packed, phone completely charged, and dark green T-shirt clinging once again to my back. I'm traveling with Dr. Patricia Melzer, our program leader, and fourteen German-speaking students from Temple. Our first few days together consisted of an introductory program in Berlin and now, with a whole month ahead of us, we begin our journey southward just days before the start of summer language school.

Leipzig is a city of many names. Some call it a *Musikstadt*, or music city, as Leipzig has served a long list of European classical musicians like Wagner, the Mendelssohns, and Mahler. At the center of its music culture lies Johann Sebastian Bach, the renowned German composer and former music director in Leipzig's St. Thomas Church. Others might call it a *Grüne Stadt*, or green city, for its vast collection of sprawling parks and placid lakes. Leipzig also ranks among Germany's most livable cities and is commonly referred to as the former heart of East Germany.

There's even one more name to include in my list.

For the next four weeks, Leipzig is home.

Our train pulls into the *Leipzig Hauptbahnhof*, or main train station, like the arrival of spring after a raw, dark winter. Temple students depart their carriages like bits of pollen thrust fancifully into the city by chilly breezes. I step out of the station into a bustling section of downtown Leipzig like the first of many trees to bloom, offering my individual contribution to what will soon be a cascade of bright colors, fresh scents, and the beauty of rebirth.

I spend the early days of this Leipzig spring settling into a communist-style apartment complex in *Lößnig*, a tiny neighborhood south of the city center. The *Grüne Stadt* proved its name quickly when I discovered my building stands next to an expansive park with grassy hills and seemingly endless meadows.

My family would be hardly surprised to learn that my favorite introductory activity occurred at a beer garden. The *Gosenschenke "Ohne Bedenken"* was the host of our first Temple-sponsored meal and quickly became one of my favorite restaurants in Leipzig. The name *Gosenschenke* means "tavern serving *Gose*," a beer known for its strong salty flavor. Though *Gose* was first brewed in central Germany, it became so popular in Leipzig that the beer is often associated with the former heart of East Germany. While I always planned to investigate the gastronomy in Leipzig, I never suspected how crucial one beer garden would be in my German studies and pursuit of English teaching fellowships.

Just as the *Gosenschenke* became the Sandinos of Leipzig, so too did Melzer adopt an analogous role to Ralph and Murph in my German studies. Often dressed in all black with glasses to match, she quickly established herself as a cross between a mother duck and bad-ass aunt. Melzer was not responsible for teaching any courses, but rather facilitated experiences outside of class and led extra excursions for all Temple students.

She welcomes me and my peers into the *Gosenschenke* beer garden on the day before the start of language school. Melzer finds our group a table and wastes no time introducing us to Leipzig's famous brew.

"I recommend everyone who is interested in learning about German beer to try at least a small glass of *Gose*."

The mention of any beer, let alone *Gose*, is more than enough motivation for our college group to swarm the outdoor taps in this picturesque beer garden. We gather under white and blue umbrellas and look around at an assortment of outdoor wooden dining tables, blossoming trees, and Germans happily munching on a collection of local dishes.

I muster my best German accent upon reaching the front of the line.

"A large *Gose* with mango please."

"Absolutely," the bartender replies, setting down a large glass under the tap while fetching a container of mango puree. He pours my beer and then tilts the glass to add a scoop of fruity goodness. I hand him some Euros and fetch my drink, eager to watch globs of mango disperse into the dark yellow *Gose*. My first sip is both salty and citric, and the fruitiness adds hints of spring to what would otherwise be an autumnal flavor. I'm already a quarter through the entire glass upon returning to our table and will be back in line before I know it.

"Let's be sure to order soon," announces Melzer, ensuring we all have menus with any necessary translations.

I run my finger down the list with no clear idea of what to pair with this unique German beer sitting on the table before me. A collection of soups, salad plates, the famous *Schweineschnitzel,* and the *Gosenschenke's* own take on *Schweinshaxe,* or pig's foot, prohibit any easy selection. My attention is eventually snared by a familiar name tucked away deep in this monster of a menu. The corresponding dish appears to be something between a salad and sandwich with the following label: *Ohne Bedenken,* like *Gosenschenke "Ohne Bedenken."*

I already know the word *ohne* means "without," but *bedenken* is foreign to my young German vocabulary.

"Hey Dr. M," I shout over a sea of students, "what's this *Ohne Bedenken* on the menu? What does it mean?"

"There are a few different translations for it," she responds. "Without thinking, without concern, without reservation. The most accurate is probably the third, without reservation. I think that dish is a mixture of all listed ingredients and flavors on one plate."

"Is this phrase just used for food?"

Melzer puts down her menu and walks over.

"Oh no, it's not unique to the dish. *Ohne Bedenken* is the idea to try new things without fear, or reservation, as to what might go wrong."

"Okay, so it's kind of a philosophy then?"

"You could say that," she responds. "It's to go with the flow and not shy away from the moment, to not let any inhibitions interfere with plans or future actions."

"Fascinating," I reply, "guess I already know what I'm ordering today!"

"It seems so," she smiles, returning to her seat.

The waiter arrives and I proudly ask for that philosophical dish named *Ohne Bedenken*.

There's a subtle distinction between attitude and the necessary energy to act on any opportunity. Attitude controls the perception of new challenges and goals in a 10 percent situation, the motivation for acceleration. What actually causes that acceleration, the impetus for acting on a *potential* 90 percent response, lies in something by a familiar name.

Ohne Bedenken is the natural successor to proper attitude. It allows one to consider all possible opportunities in any 10 percent situation and then facilitates the most promising 90 percent response. Attitude gave me the chance to study German, and though I may not have realized as much in 2018, I used *Ohne Bedenken* to justify a leap of faith on Leipzig, complete my first German course at Temple, and begin my second study abroad program in Europe.

I arrived in Leipzig with almost all six tools for navigating change: passion, dissent, holistic international education, relationships, attitude. After studying the menu with Melzer, I began my first meal at the *Gosenschenke "Ohne Bedenken"* with the sixth ingredient sitting on the table in front of me. It goes by the name of *Ohne Bedenken* and ties together elements of the other five tools for navigating change like a finely wrapped bow on top of any birthday present.

Ohne Bedenken is the catalyst for pursuing passions, engaging in dissent, holistically examining a foreign society, and building new relationships. I can trace it through many consequential turning points and leaps of faith in the past decade. *Ohne Bedenken* facilitated Rinaldi's commitment to ice hockey, my energetic preparation for a second PMEA audition, registration for *Dissent in America*, the development of new relationships within the ice hockey community, and my pivot from engineering to German. In looking back on Leipzig, I realized *Ohne Bedenken* was just the force I needed to leave my comfort zone, learn German as an infant among native speakers, and apply for English teaching fellowships.

I already spoke at great length about building metaphorical bridges after Northern Ireland, ones which first extended from Philadelphia to Derry and Liberty to *Dissent in America*. My new trip to Leipzig then sparked the construction of another from Philadelphia to Europe in the following theme: *Sprachen bauen Brücken,* or "languages build bridges."

Our Leipzig program is literally called "languages build bridges." Although Ralph already joked about my career as a civil engineer, I don't think he could have anticipated another round of bridge construction through language learning. Maybe the Germans knew we were metaphorically building bridges in Derry, who knows. It seems my fate as an engineer, dare I pivot back, is already decided.

I conclude my first meal at the *Gosenschenke "Ohne Bedenken"* with one final sip of my *Gose*, the Guinness of Leipzig, and jitters for the first week of classes. The poker game of this new adventure is set, cards shuffled, and bets placed. I sit down at the table with only one thought in mind. Deal me in, I'm ready.

DIE DREIVIERTELSTUNDE

I crack my eyes open and wince at the clamor of screeching brakes. I stagger out of my seat, grab my backpack, and sleepwalk to an exit on this steamy tram car. My backpack is a sponge for sweat on another sweltering day in June 2019.

I step out of the *Straßenbahn*, or tram, with a brief yawn and survey my surroundings. The *Nordplatz* station has the usual hustle and bustle of a weekday morning with passengers scattering here and there, some heading north in the direction of the veterinarian's office, others treading south toward the acclaimed *Zoo Leipzig*. I trek west, strolling down *Lumumbastraße* with the odors of German flora enticing my nose along the way.

A quick walk deposits me at the door of *Lumumbastraße 4*, the home of Leipzig's *interDaF* German language school. It's another day in *Sprachen bauen Brücken* and the thrill of my upcoming class transforms my weariness into excitement. I enter the back door, climb a flight of steps, and look down the long, cream-colored hallway that hosts all language classrooms. Towering glass windows flood the walkway with comforting doses of natural morning light. I slowly walk down the hallway and pass morning traditions at language school: students wander all about, tiny samplings of German, English, and other languages implant themselves in the steady ear, bulletin boards display hand-stapled information on the upcoming excursion to Erfurt and cultural events in Leipzig.

My journey ends at the entrance to room number eight. Its open door leads me into the square classroom and I sit down in the far side near two windows. Our teacher's black, heavy desk and a towering green chalkboard lie to my left. The eight students in our A1.2 class, a level designated for beginners but not first-time German students, come from different schools and countries. Many represent Temple, others are from the University of Kansas. We even have two adult students, one from Florida and the other from Japan.

Herr Tom Heinich, our main instructor, arrives promptly at 9:00. He enters quickly, places his bag of class materials on the desk, and pauses to consider our activities for the day. There's no sign of sweat on his well-fitted black T-shirt or along his tan brow. Tom must take the heat better than I do.

He looks up gently, scanning our faces.

"Hello students, good morning. How was your project work yesterday?"

One of the primary focuses in our A1.2 course is to learn past tense and Tom wastes no time in finding creative means to practice the necessary grammatical forms. The activities vary greatly: short presentations, history lessons about prominent Germans like Martin Luther, physical flyswatter competitions for matching a *Partizip II*, or past participle, with its helping verb, relay-like text transcriptions for the grand prize of German chocolate, plus bragging rights.

We also have German phonetic classes in the afternoon and take part in special cultural projects for the entirety of our four-week program. Each group researches an aspect of life in Leipzig and we're apparently going to have some form of final performance. I was lucky to snag a spot in none other than a group entitled *Musikstadt Leipzig,* but it is not yet clear what we'll be doing for our oral presentation. Enough with the project though; Tom's prepared quite a class for today! "Students," he says as we move along through our activities, "I have one last question before break at 10:30." Tom strides over to the massive green chalkboard and picks up a short piece of chalk. Gently raising his arm to chest level, he begins inscribing a new question onto the dry surface, dictating with great deliberation. Each letter takes leaps and bounds in never-ending circles as the chalk grinds, cracks, and scrapes along the surface. Words form like eloquent speech rolls off the tongue and are bound by the intentions of their speaker, or in this case, a piece of white calcite.

Tom steps away from the board to briefly admire the dashing streaks and twirls before turning back to us.

"*Wie viele Minuten sind in einer Dreiviertelstunde?*"

He articulates the question as gracefully as written.

"Any ideas?" Tom gazes from right to left at what is a full class today.

His question is met by silence. It stretches and widens, filling the entire room with similar anticipation to Balmages' piano soliloquy all those years ago. We wait in a grand pause with Tom as our conductor. Beads of sweat depart my brow and trickle down a freshly-shaved cheek; they're not just from the heat.

Ok, I wonder, *this question sounds vaguely familiar, but what the hell is that last word?*

Tom asks again.

"*Wie viele Minuten sind in einer Dreiviertelstunde?*"

I sit frozen to my chair, perplexed by my inability to decipher his new query. In this moment of frustration, my thoughts wander back to a text from recent memory.

Hello Roger Williams.

Learning a foreign language requires scientific dissection of the unknown. There is nothing more effective than chipping away at unfamiliar words and phrases without reservation, fighting through the thickness of some gray fog to discover everything concealed within it. Peer teaching required the fearless pursuit of texts like Williams' *Tenent* with my students, and the same mentality applies for learning German.

In other words, it's time for *Ohne Bedenken.*

Wie, I think, *that's how. Viele means many, and yes, Minuten is minutes.*

Looks like einer means the letter "a" in the dative case and it's paired with the word sind meaning are.

Hmm, perhaps I can break up this next word.

Dreiviertelstunde. Damn that's long. Stunde should be the word for hour, makes sense with the bit about Minuten for minutes.

I tap my pencil on my workbook and look for some kind of clue in their occasional collision. Tom waits silently at the front of the room. Our class guesses not a word as the minutes drag on.

Let's see: Dreiviertelstunde = Dreiviertel+Stunde.

But Dreiviertel?

Drei means three, so maybe it's Drei+Viertel+Stunde.

Three-something-hour.

Oh, I don't know, how exactly could this relate to minutes?

My mind flashes back to German I at Temple.

What about viertel vor and viertel nach? I think they mean quarter before and quarter after. Okay, so maybe Viertel is quarter. Not a living quarter, but literally a quarter. 1/4. 25 percent. Let's run with that.

It's almost 10:30. Someone has to get this before break. *Drei+Viertel+Stunde = Three+Quarter+Hour. There we have it, a three-quarter hour, or forty-five minutes!* A smile streaks across my face.

"Tom," I exclaim, "there's forty-five minutes in a three-quarter hour!"

"Very good Adam, forty-five minutes indeed."

He responds with a wink and dismisses us for our break.

This class with Tom reinforced one of the most crucial lessons for any young German student: the language overflows with compound words. They are sometimes quite difficult to decipher but there is often a logic to their construction and meaning. My first German professor at Temple described it as follows: speaking German is like playing with Legos. Grab the right pieces, understand how they fit together, and use your creativity. Then, before you know it, you've made something beautiful.

I waltz out of *Lumumbastraße 4* with a spring in my step and the morning sun on my back. My route takes me one block north and then in the direction of the *Handwerksbäckerei Kleinert* for an apple cake and cappuccino. I sit down on a wooden bench in a nearby park with my spoils of victory over the *Dreiviertelstunde.*

The gears are finally starting to turn, patterns revealing themselves, compound constructions becoming more familiar. I might be the newest German speaker from Temple on this trip, and my performance in this course might be extremely influential in my future plans, but these early classes in Leipzig are the first sign that my pivot toward German and fellowships might actually bear fruit. Moments like these with Tom bring me back to Scheidly's yearbook quote from high school, the idea that symbols, whether German letters or mathematical operators, are *language*. I never expected to find a connection between foreign languages and science but believe the link between these passions, like my combination of music and ice hockey in officiating, is what has made this German journey feel so right in its first six months.

Each new opportunity in class and on the streets of Leipzig reveals the increasing usefulness of *Ohne Bedenken* in my lingual pursuits. At its core, *Ohne Bedenken* is another means to say "Dammit, let's do this job and do it right. Hold nothing back and have no regrets." It is only without reservation that I can piece together incoherent samplings of German and extract meaning out of them. *Ohne Bedenken* snowballs my excitement for language learning and fascination with German into the very forces I'll need to be successful in Leipzig and with my English teaching applications.

Outside of group meals at the *Gosenschenke "Ohne Bedenken,"* there were three primary aspects of *Sprachen bauen Brücken*. I just experienced one in the classroom and another is the completion of the *Musikstadt Leipzig* group project. While these two components were critical in learning the German language, some of the most useful tests of my lingual skills occurred far outside the classroom.

Our group from Temple completed many excursions during our time in Leipzig that, like the previously mentioned trip to Erfurt, gave us a well-rounded perspective of eastern Germany. Melzer might have not used the word as we know it, but the theme of holistic international education was ever-present in my travels around Leipzig. Though she strongly encouraged group trips, Melzer, as Ralph did in Derry, often supported individual exploration to build our language skills and self-confidence.

Solo excursions in and outside of Leipzig were the third and equally useful part of my German studies that summer, and just as *Ohne Bedenken* played a critical role in my classroom experiences with Tom, so too was it at the heart of expanding my comfort zone in the German world. This coffee and apple cake break after the *Dreiviertelstunde* is one of many occasions when I researched opportunities to challenge my basic lingual skills and learn more about Germany. A new journey outside of Leipzig awaits me soon enough, but not before a quick glance at my phone interrupts my plans for the future. The morning break only lasts thirty minutes and I can't be late to class. I grin after checking my digital clock.

10:45, I chuckle to myself. Now that's a *Dreiviertelstunde*.

WITTENBERG

Bitte einsteigen und die Türen schließen!

I turn around for one last look at the *Leipzig Hauptbahnhof* before entering a regional express. The high, arched glass mimics giant church windows while the hustle of travelers and railway attendants foreshadows today's destination. Another conductor repeats the same German phrase as above, motioning for passengers to board quickly before all doors close.

It is now over a week since Melzer led our group excursion to Erfurt, a medieval German city spared by Allied bombing during World War II. This Saturday in late June will deviate significantly from that trip, as I'm finally traveling solo to a town for the ages.

Wittenberg lies approximately seventy kilometers north of Leipzig. It occupies the northern bank of the Elbe, a river conjuring grandiose memories from the famous meeting between American and Soviet forces near Torgau at the end of World War II. I'm drawn to this small German town to satisfy my interests in language learning and history. Wittenberg was at the center of early European dissent that I first studied with Ralph in 2016 and then relearned with Tom only weeks ago. Exploration along the Elbe will also offer opportunities to practice my language skills in the theme of *Ohne Bedenken*.

Smashed gravel churns under my rugged boots after I exit the *Wittenberg Hauptbahnhof.* I quickly reach the city limits and confront a peculiar stillness. Gravel transitions to smooth cobblestones in barren streets lined with the regional flag of Saxony. Picturesque flower baskets spring up from an assortment of rainbow-colored houses as restaurants advertise regional beers in front of empty seats and tables.

The only signs of life in this ghost town are inklings of music in the distance. I adjust my route and follow the sound, intrigued by what might be, of all things, American jazz. My ears confirm this surprise after finding the *Innenstadt*, or city center: it really is jazz, just with a German twist.

I enter a bustling town square and discover the *Rathaus*, or town hall. It's surrounded by bikes with metal baskets, a carousel, decorated buildings, and carnival tents. Middle school musicians occupy a makeshift stage and taunt my ears with American classics in front of an eager audience of parents and friends. I look into the middle of the square and spot a statue of Martin Luther, his face undisturbed by the activities all around him.

Welcome to the 2019 *Luther Hochzeit*, a Renaissance-themed festival with musicians, craftsmen, food stands, clothing vendors, dancing, and interactive demonstrations. Martin Luther was already mentioned in class with Tom and is one of the first European protesters discussed in *Dissent in America*. Luther was an extremely influential German priest, monk, and professor who made his mark on European history during the early 16th century. (Encyclopaedia Britannica Online Ed, Luther, 2021) This year's festival in Wittenberg marks the 494th celebration of Luther's *Hochzeit*, or marriage, to Katherine of Bora. The pair got married in 1525. (Encyclopaedia Britannica Online Ed, Luther, 2021)

Luther is well-known for publishing his *Ninety-five Theses* on October 31st, 1517. He used this document to dissent against certain practices and beliefs held by the Catholic Church. His protest sparked the Protestant Reformation, a process which ostracized Luther from Catholicism and led to the subsequent development of Christian sects. (Encyclopaedia Britannica Online Ed, Luther, 2021) Luther's dissent rippled through space and time in the coming centuries and the beginning of American colonial history was influenced by the aftermath of German protest against Rome. (National Geographic Society, 2021)

In addition to sending his *Theses* to the Archbishop of Mainz and the Bishop of Brandenburg, Luther possibly stapled them to the door of the All Saints' Church, or the *Schlosskirche,* in downtown Wittenberg as a physical mark of his dissent. (Encyclopaedia Britannica Online Ed, Ninety-five, 2021) Although I did not know the exact location of Wittenberg before coming to Germany, the town became a must-visit after I discovered its close proximity to Leipzig. Better yet, upon realizing that the All Saints' Church still stands to this day, I had no choice but to navigate through the *Hochzeit* celebration and find that legendary door.

I approach the scene of Luther's supposed dissent as the sun blankets every tightly packed street in Wittenberg with simmering heat. The All Saints' Church lies at the very western edge of the *Innenstadt,* a Gothic monument which contrasts from relatively modernized buildings around it. Luther's door is located next to the main tower and underneath a mural of Jesus; it is massive, metallic, and constrained between a stone and marble frame. Luther's *Theses* are engraved in six columns on the current replica; a plaque on the door indicates that the original unfortunately burned down in the 18th century.

A kind German woman takes my picture in front of the *Theses* before I step back and consider this new leg in my journey through dissent. Luther's legacy was cemented after one defiant moment, from a single treatise that irrevocably changed the world. Spiraling out of his contempt towards the Catholic Church came a power struggle within Christianity, waves of emigration from Europe, and new translations of the Bible. Modern religious practices and national identities are further testament to the impact of Luther's singular dissent. (Encyclopaedia Britannica Online Ed, Protestantism, 2021)

History is alive on the streets of Wittenberg. This *Hochzeit* festival, along with the protests and bonfires of Derry, is a reminder that yesterday's actions will shape the destiny of millions. Luther, like characters in my life, took a leap of faith on his beliefs and convictions. You or I need not be German religious dissenters to take a chance on the future we desire, and if Luther's story proves one thing, it's that you never quite know where your moments of bravery, determination, and investment in yourself will take us all. While Rinaldi's vision brought him into the hockey community and Ivy's perseverance began her path to one (eventually successful!) Fulbright application, my own dissent sent me to Germany. We all have roles to play in this drama called humanity and can make our impact with one leap of faith at a time, through the swing of a sword or stroke of a pen.

Grumbles from my stomach and the smell of roasting meats are enough temptation to pull me back into the festival. I peruse different vendors, stands, and attractions, snapping pictures of anything from assortments of cured sausages to Renaissance-style street performers. The entirety of Wittenberg, plus tourists, must be crammed into this town's few major walkways as I duck and swerve through German-speaking crowds. Unfamiliar words, phrases, and exclamations pass in and out of both ears and provoke my interest in language learning at every turn.

I travel eastwards before wandering into one of the many tucked-away alleys that make European cities so fascinating to explore. Medieval music greets me as I walk under a mossy stone archway into a tiny, circular courtyard. I wanted to find gifts for the family during my time abroad and am captivated by a quaint pottery stand. It offers plates, silverware, jugs, chalices, mugs, carafes, garden displays, stools, abstract pieces; you name it, I found it.

A set of ceramic cups immediately snags my attention. Melzer gave us a historical lesson during one of our group meals on this specific ceramic mug, or *Becher*, that was used to drink wine in olden times. They are cylindrical at the bottom and gradually curve outwards with increasing height.

I wave my hand and catch the stand owner's attention. Careful preparation already supplied me with the necessary vocabulary, verbs, and grammatical forms for my impending purchase. I'm ready to use my skills on the street, to expand on my classwork with Tom and the *Dreiviertelstunde*. I will successfully navigate this German conversation with Luther's city as my witness.

"Hello!" she welcomes me. "What can I help you with?"

I point down to the *Becher*. "I'd like four of these please."

"Excellent choice," she replies, reaching down to collect the cups.

"Wait," I interject, "can I put these *Becher* in the dishwasher?" They're covered in a rather thick glaze and it never hurts to ask.

She scratches her chin before responding.

"Can you *what* with them?"

"Um," I stutter, "are they machine washable?"

"What?"

My brain puckers at her confusion. Neuron blasts away in search of anything to quell this misunderstanding.

I said washable, can I wash them, what is wrong with that? Is it my accent? Poor grammar?

There's an even more sinister possibility. The term "false friends" is used to describe words that appear similarly in the German and English languages but do not share the same meaning. One classic example:

English: the gift = *das Geschenk*

German: *das Gift* = the poison

In other words, the gift ≠ *das Gift*

The only poisons in this conversation are my apparently insufficient lingual skills. My mind identifies two *possible* false friends who might just be ruining this moment in Wittenberg.

The German verbs *wachsen* and *waschen* are almost identical in appearance and completely different in pronunciation. One means "to wash" and the other "to grow," their definitions separated by the guttural-sounding "achs" and English-sounding "asch." Though *waschen*, literally spelled like "wash," would naturally make sense, it's *wachsen* that means "to wash" and *waschen* a false friend.

I can definitely, well maybe, recall a lecture where *wachsen* was clarified as "to wash." I've studied my notes, prepared for this conversation, and pursued it with *Ohne Bedenken*.

Wachsen, it has to be right. Probably.

I fill the naked silence with another insistence on *wachsen*.

"Can I wash these with a machine?"

She stares back with no change in expression. My heart rate plummets with each passing second and descends into free-fall like my first few weeks at Temple. *Hochzeit* festivities continue all around us.

Could it really be waschen?

She eventually returns a heartbeat to our conversation.

"Perhaps you mean *waschen?*"

God dammit.

"Yeah, maybe so." I deflate like a balloon from Luther's bachelor party.

"Well of course then," she mumbles, "of course they're machine *wash*able."

A handful of awkward seconds elapse before she finishes wrapping the *Becher.* I pass her the necessary Euros and take my package like a scolded child.

There's nothing like a slap in the face from one's inabilities with a foreign language. It doesn't matter how many courses I've taken, videos I've watched, and times I've succeeded in the classroom: I'll never be able to grow a *Becher.* One of the most sophisticated skills with foreign languages is to take theory and apply it on the street, and today's experience in Wittenberg proved I am far from that level of independence with German. To imagine such competence in six months is simply foolish.

The only false friends in my encounter were overconfidence and the assumption that *Ohne Bedenken* will solve every problem, always deliver the right answer so long as I pursue truth without reservation. It cannot and will not control someone else's reaction to my 90 percent decision, regardless if I'm speaking my own language or a foreign one.

This moment at the *Becher* stand was one of many in Germany where I, for the first time in my life, felt the embarrassment of an outsider lacking control over the native tongue. I'll never personally know how it feels to be a foreigner in the United States, a land which simultaneously praises and demonizes immigration, but today was one of many chances to experience the insecurity of an outsider looking inwards.

Our conversation demonstrates the second form of language learning in Leipzig, the opportunity to test lingual skills with ordinary Germans. Mastering these interactions is one of my greatest hurdles to overcome and often requires more than attitude and *Ohne Bedenken*. However, there is a saving grace to letdowns like the great *wachsen* debate. My struggles with German are akin to my most important takeaway from PMEA auditions: failure builds the framework for success. A 90 percent response without reservation will always serve me well, but it sometimes takes a cup or two of failure to finish the recipe for speaking German in Germany. Each and every blunder is preparation for an eventual breakthrough, that shining moment when theoretical grammar discussions with Tom translate to casual German conversations. Just being here to make mistakes is the beauty of this study abroad experience, for there's no better place to fail than a land where the next opportunity to speak comes in seconds, not days or weeks.

I depart the hidden courtyard with my *Becher* and embrace my struggles on the streets of Wittenberg. Though the failings of a young German student are bound to bog me down, I can still find moments to appreciate the connections between this summer and my past adventures. *Sprachen bauen Brücken* is amassing familiar friends under an umbrella called German: language learning with Scheidly, studying Martin Luther with Ralph, pursuing holism in Derry, building relationships within new communities.

The final test of my German skills awaits me in the *Musikstadt Leipzig* presentation and conquering such a speaking task will be no easy feat. If today's experience was like my first PMEA audition, then I pray *Musikstadt* will be like my second.

My last stroll around the Wittenberg *Innenstadt* leads me back to the All Saints' Church. I find Luther's door, take one final picture, decide to climb the church tower. The lookout at the top greets me with a noncommittal breeze and rumblings from the *Hochzeit* down below.

The skyline bleeds on this night meant for sunsets, painting Wittenberg like a citrus fruit. I lean gently on the tower wall and spot the Elbe glistening under such a romantic sky. I envision it sparkling beyond the banks of Luther's town, propelled forward to a destination which is uncertain and from a source it does not know. The Elbe wanders into the distance like my path back to Leipzig, flowing steadily towards the inviting horizon and a future waiting in the beyond.

DAS ORCHESTER

There is a fascinating relationship between practice and performance. They are simultaneously both interdependent and separate, two parts of one whole that rely on each other while maintaining a distinct, if not foreign, distance.

I already mentioned at PMEA All-States that musicians must "practice like they perform" and master all aspects of a composition before displaying their final product. However, experienced performers will tell you that, no matter how many hours have been invested in repetitive preparation, performances are different from practice.

There is the audience, potential feelings of so-called "performance anxiety," and the damnable knowledge that one's actions are final. Performances permit no do-overs, no second occasion to right one's wrongs. Life offers only a finite number of chances to utilize our opportunities, should we have the courage to act on them.

I plop down in the basement of the *Moritzbastei*, a restaurant in downtown Leipzig that boasts an underground seating area and stage. The brick-lined room bubbles with energy while its cool, refreshing atmosphere is readily heated by the entire *Sprachen bauen Brücken* community in late June 2019. Bright lights illuminate caramel-colored wooden panels on stage, ones which invite the attention of over one hundred German students and teachers bound between towering arches and a chilly cement floor. I wait by the far back wall with the members of *Musikstadt Leipzig,* folding both arms in front of my chest as I await our final group presentation.

Taking a leap of faith on German was no simple task, and this crucial performance will either make or break my trajectory towards English teaching fellowships. Everything is on the line: my pride, confidence, reputation among all my peers and teachers, validation after championing opportunities abroad over those numbers. I completed my fair share of practice, used every meal at the *Gosenschenke,* productive class with Tom, and solo excursion to improve my language skills. Yet, despite all my prior experiences with musical and officiating performances, today's challenge reeks of an incredibly foul odor. The smell swamps my entire body, starting first in the nose and then trickling down every nerve ending to a sudden thud in my feet as *Musikstadt Leipzig* heads backstage.

Our performance will highlight Leipzig's rich music history and the famous musicians who once called the city home. It only takes five minutes to transform ourselves into classical musicians with white powder wigs, fake glasses, and even a cardboard time machine. One student has assumed the role of Johann Sebastian Bach and will use that time machine to visit Mendelssohn, Mahler, and all the other musicians featured in the yearbook of Leipzig's past. I will imitate Richard Wagner, the German composer famous for his bombastic operas and contributions during the Romantic Era. My prepared dialogue describes his life, relationship with Leipzig, and famous compositions like "Ride of the Valkyries." I specifically grew out my sideburns for this performance and am ready, even if to my own demise, to mimic Wagner as closely as possible.

My stomach convulses as showtime draws near. Caffeine from my morning coffee sprints through every vein and aggravates my heart rate far above normal rhythm in this sauna of a dressing room.

"Hey," I mention to members of our group, "I'll be right back, gotta, I gotta hit the bathroom."

I pace around the empty underground lavatory and stop to look up in a mirror.

Uh, got to fix my hair!

I run my hand through my bangs several times.

Sideburns are okay, glad I didn't grow Wagner's neck beard, but the bangs fell again. More gel would've helped.

Moisture weighs down my back like an anchor. My amber-colored shirt bleeds clear, revealing sweat to match my oily hands and face.

Agh, the hair again? Need to retuck my shirt.

Someone knocks on the door. "We're almost ready, you good?"

"Gimme one second!" I shout while backing away from the mirror.

I grab my head as German lines project like 35 mm film on the walls around me. Wagner's early works and most famous operas blend with the German pronunciation of "Ride of the Valkyries," not to mention the details of my walk out onto the stage and how I desperately need Bach to understand my first line because the entire school will be watching and, ideally, not notice how sweaty I already am at the start.

Breathe, kid. Breathe.

Another impatient knock draws me back to our team. We organized our performance to run chronologically, sampling from Leipzig's earliest to most contemporary musicians.

Wagner enters near the end of our presentation and I stand tensely as other students ascend the stage with Bach.

Remember PMEA States? You're no stranger to solo performance.

Composers from all different musical eras speak with Bach before I receive the final nod from another group member. I take two huge breaths, duck under an archway, and stroll out into the spotlight.

I enter from stage right and conceal my notes in a folder covered with music staffs. The air is surprisingly dry against my saturated skin in this cool, subterranean basement.

Bach pauses and I counter his inaction by moving to center stage. I glance over at my paper, though it'll do little good. My vision smears the German lines into a chaotic assortment of music notes. I run my eyes back and forth across the text as I take a fake pen in hand and feign the construction of some musical composition on my folder. The audience briefly chuckles before withdrawing to a sea of whispers.

The writing stops, pen falls silent, folder slightly lowers. I look out into the crowd like a conductor before his orchestra, holding my baton of a pen at the ready. I know Tom and Melzer are out there somewhere, staring down my every move as I turn to the white-haired figure of Bach.

My right foot inches forward, then the left, each step carrying less weight than its predecessor. The wood on stage has given way to clouds. I might as well be floating.

Bach and I stand across from each other in empty, naked silence. He waits for my signal, the beginning of our predetermined conversation. I pause, open mouthed, debating whether to make a sound.

Bach stares. I look right back.

The stage splits down the middle and forms a chasm between me and my partner. My body glistens under the artificial stage lights as I look across the misty abyss, gazing at the spoils of my potential success. There lies a smiling Bach, finished English teaching applications, and the satisfaction of having used my practice to perform without regret. Oh what I would give to greet my partner on the other side of this gorge, hear his joyful responses in dialogue, and touch those finalized fellowship essays in the soft, winding grooves of my hands.

All I need to do is jump. Leap, without reservation.

Ohne Bedenken, I smile, *you lead the way.*

"Hello Bach!"

Our conversation is electric from the start. Each carefully constructed sentence is one step into the future, driven by none other than the will to *act without reserve*, to paint a portrait of two musicians in the theme of *Ohne Bedenken*. Bach and I speak without fear of failure, rejection, or that this crowd might rip me to shreds in a language I knew not six months ago. I describe my passion for music and highlight how dissent led to some of my artistic accomplishments. We give life to German music history with details from our personal experiences, famous compositions, and specific contributions to Leipzig. Every sentence develops our relationship as Bach and I maintain a positive attitude and purse the proper 90 percent response to any error or hiccup.

The rest of *Musikstadt Leipzig* comes out onto the stage after we finish our dialogue. They join us under the spotlight and we form a line with Bach at the center. I position myself to the right of Bach, withdraw a crinkled piece of sheet music from my folder, and turn toward the pianist. He gives us our cue and *Musikstadt Leipzig* begins its performance of *Das Orchester*, or the orchestra. The piece is written in four-part harmony and describes the standard orchestra in German. I sing alone on the bass part, booming from the bottom-most depths of my voice.

We mimic the Berlin Philharmonic in the basement of Leipzig's *Moritzbastei*. *Das Orchester* radiates outward from the stage and ripples through the air, bouncing off every brick, wooden panel, seat, student, and teacher while the bright stage lights illuminate our smiling faces. I stand upright as our singing prompts reflection from high school, college, and study abroad. Music has the special ability to connect past and present and our performance funnels my memories as follows:

High school experiences yielding passions for the arts, athletics, and academics
Undergraduate journey transformed by dissent against initial plans
Custom blend of ice hockey and music in officiating
Studying abroad twice in Europe
The German language
Das Orchester

Today's performance is about much more than Bach or the Musikstadt.
Leipzig was hiding what I was searching for all along.
I found my song to sing.

Das Orchester is met with enthusiastic applause from our peers and instructors. I soak in these final moments like a sponge and bask in the realization that the German language is my numbers. Each word is a mathematical operator, every sentence a line of code. These sentences then form paragraphs, entire essays, and give birth to thought in a programming language like no other. Just as officiating fills the gaps between hockey and music, so too does the German language link the chain between my engineering studies and quest to teach English in Europe. It confirms Scheidly's inscription of *language* and transcends the barriers between those who interpret the world through different tongues. In learning to think like a foreign people, I opened the door to new relationships, international journeys, and performances on stage in the *Musikstadt*.

Sprachen bauen Brücken assembled all my tools for navigating change: passion, dissent, holistic international education, relationships, attitude, *Ohne Bedenken*. They stand ready at my disposal and are equally available for you. While a commitment to German brought me my song to sing, the question still remaining is what you will do with your next leap of faith. New activities, jobs, relationships? Maybe even a song or two?

I know not what lies on your horizon but want to emphasize the following point about preparing for any new endeavor: overcoming some challenges will be harder than taking your leap(s) of faith on them. Be prepared to pursue a better future because you believe in it and know you're ready to invest the necessary time and energy. My decision to study German brought on a whole new set of obstacles in my life, and I only encountered success in the *Moritzbastei* after sustained dedication to language learning.

Though I may leave Leipzig in June 2019 as a relative nobody in the worlds of German and English teaching, I can feel the wind in my sails guiding me back to Europe after graduation. My compass points no direction other than forward, to higher levels of German, fellowship applications, teaching my native language, and giving back for all I've experienced this summer. My transformation from a lost engineering student to a proud German speaker is complete, and while the daunting task of writing applications awaits me upon my return to the United States, I will face my post-collegiate goals in the familiar theme of *Ohne Bedenken.*

I now present a newly updated form of the equation first encountered in Fall 2018:

Hockey + Music + Physics + Dissent
+ Derry + Officiating
+ Mechanical Engineering + German = ?

The geographical answer to that question mark lies well beyond my experiences in the *Moritzbastei,* and while I still have the chance, I'd like to take these last few moments in Leipzig to amend the statement at the beginning of this study abroad program.

Maybe Twain was right, maybe it was impossible to learn German in Germany. To hell with that though, I found a *Musikstadt* with evidence to the contrary. My personal revision of his opening quote is as follows:

I don't believe there is anything in the whole earth that you can't learn in Leipzig, including the German language.

THE YEAR LIKE
NO OTHER

THE AMERICA I KNOW

The America I know is enduring a year like no other.

I gaze out from the back left passenger seat in my mom's SUV. Her car glides over familiar bumps on the Pennsylvania Turnpike as I stare out at the exit signs. The regular list floats by like dandelions in the wind:

Norristown, Philadelphia Ambler, Doylestown Jenkintown, Bensalem, Street Road

Every off-ramp reveals the same signs and missing spots of paint. When I was younger, I would eagerly wait for the exits, wondering if today might be the day when they would no longer abide by the usual names and numbers. I was biding my time for that inevitable surprise, a rush of excitement from some variation in routine commutes with my mom.

Different signs, renamed exits, perhaps a whole new turnpike?

Nothing. The signs never changed, but I kept on waiting.

My brother sits to my right, his chaotic head of hair tamed into gelled waves of brown, while my dad sits shotgun and mom in the driver's seat. Suitcases bounce around the trunk in unison with the occasional change in road material. A light gray sky sketches sentimental clouds on the car's reflective exterior while my mom drives in turbo mode to the Pennsylvania border.

Welcome to September 2020. It's over a full year since *Das Orchester* filled the airwaves in Leipzig's *Moritzbastei* and my time at Temple University is officially over. Last fall I began my final year of undergraduate study, an experience I anticipated since elementary school but never believed would actually happen. My last year of college, in the flesh. Impossible.

The few months after Leipzig were dominated by writing fellowship applications with Ivy, Barbara, Melzer, and Ralph. I enrolled in German III and took Temple's German IV in the following semester. My final engineering courses and senior design project were in full swing and I could practically taste the champagne after commencement ceremonies in May 2020.

I spent a good deal of time in Fall 2019 with Ivy, Luke, Rinaldi, and other friends at Temple. There was still much work to be done, but it was a celebratory time, one which begged us students to enjoy our final year together. Weekly meals in Chinatown, officiating college hockey on the weekends, exploring Philadelphia one neighborhood at a time— that was the life.

I had great optimism for the future at the beginning of my last semester. Final exams, projects, spring break, and graduation; my peers and I were in the end game with nothing left to stop us, or so we thought.

Everything changed in the America I know on March 13th, 2020. I will carry that date with me till death do us part.

Friday the 13th.

My first actual Tinder date.

Temple's last day of in-person classes.

The great wheel of society ground to a halt on March 13th and ceded to the most powerful breaking force known to man. There was no war, no alien invasion, no natural disaster.

March 13th was a day for movies, for all those films that test our will to believe the unbelievable. It was a day for doctors and nurses, for all those who devote their careers to saving lives. It was also a day for writers, for all those who print and distribute impossible musings about the future.

Most importantly, March 13th was a day for liars, fiction, and made-up names. Only one word does the date true justice. Pandemic.

**

Empty streets and full houses. Two opposites that somehow attract. My memories from March to May 2020, the so-called "quarantine," are more like dreams than reality.

I grew up on a small hill and was always fascinated by the intersection below the steeper side of our street. A walk down from our house reveals a fork in the road, a y-shaped junction between opposite paths around the base of the hill. Both streets were always bustling with traffic and no place for kids or even the most courageous biker.

They became two empty streets on March 13th, 2020. The houses around them were suddenly full, overflowing with energetic anxiety. The busyness of that y-shaped intersection infused itself into every neighboring home, driving one family at a time into longing for a "return to normal," "new normal," anything reminiscent of that unusually desirable word. Normal.

A heavy snowfall in the weeks after March 13th turned my dreams into reality. I walked down the hill with my brother, looked out into the white stillness, and placed one foot into the intersection. No horns beeped, not a single car swerved to avoid me. My second foot landed and there was still silence.

Then came the biggest thrill of all: riding that yellow line between two lanes like it's the rule, not the exception. I placed both feet where the paint rested under several inches of snow and surveyed my surroundings. You never realize how a road looks until you step into it, and as I gazed at the white stillness all around us, an eeriness overtook me and my brother.

How long would our footprints last?

Hours, days? Even weeks?

Who could say in a time of empty streets.

***

The America I know grew restless in the summer. Those full houses emptied onto vacant streets in early June 2020, bringing the impatient nation to a reckoning on its identity not seen for decades. The floodgates were lifted, and the ensuing deluge might have been the only thing spreading faster than the pandemic.

I recall broken necks, red hats, and the tear-gassed faces of Americans fighting for the rights we hold to be self-evident. That summer was a wake-up call, a reminder of Ralph's thesis that America is defined by dissent. I watched American versus American in moral combat on the streets, preaching opposite tales about the utter ineptitude of our national response to a disease not enough of us believed in and few would hopefully contract. The deaths kept ticking on up and I don't just mean from the virus.

Every day brought new struggles in a campaign against the division sowed by some of the highest powers in the land. Television headlines could not keep pace when America said hold up, this just ain't right. And so the protests continued.

I saw Americans fighting for accountability, the belief in science, and representation that dissolves polarization, not emboldens it. I saw Americans fighting both for and against our most basic instincts, a war between primal nationalism and the notion we are a beacon to the world and should start acting like it. I saw Americans fighting to come together, to resist the pandemic of misinformation that swept the land with conspiracy theories, fake news, and alternate realities. As the days went on, I saw Americans fighting to prove the America I know still exists at all.

***

Another pair of bumps brings me and my family to the Delaware River Bridge. I look out my window once again, this time at the shimmering water down below. Ahead lies the New Jersey Turnpike, one of the most congested and depressing roads on the eastern seaboard.

The river is bordered on both sides by construction sights and cranes of all different heights. Flags abusing America's sacred colors dangle from the top of several booms, banners proclaiming greatness and the need to maintain said superiority at any cost necessary. I watched them drift in the breeze and bake under the afternoon sun before we crossed into New Jersey. Those flags were out of sight but never out of mind.

To call America great is both a truth and a lie.

A truth because it is an amazing product of dissent, democratic ideals, and dreams for a brighter future since the late 18th century. A lie because it isn't, because a dissection of our past proves the America we want to believe in has failings in large supply. Just like those construction sights, the America I know has been a work in progress since its first day on the job, or the time of dissenters like Roger Williams.

I heard two arguments in the summer of empty houses and full streets. Some claimed any mention of our country's faults directly equates to hating America. They demanded love to be binding and unconditional; all attempts to find truths which hurt our national image are equivalent to treason.

Then came the opposite perspective. They maintained those arguments of "love" couldn't be any further from the truth, for loving one's country requires acknowledgment of its successes and sins.

I have questions for them both.

Have you ever heard of the Second Amendment? The land of the free and the brave and horrific mass shootings?

Have you ever heard of the great melting pot with a wall along the southern border?

Have you ever heard of democracy, civil liberties, and world leadership in the same land plagued by slavery, segregation, and the savage treatment of native people?

Like I found with the protests, bonfires, and duality in Northern Ireland, we only know America by understanding all our goodness and evils. It's only after accepting the past and present that we, as Americans, can begin to cherish our virtues and remedy our vices.

What makes America great is that it's not, not yet anyway. The quest to reach our founding ideals, the American quest, is the path to said greatness. It is coming together to understand and welcome this journey that truly makes us exceptional, and the America I know stands at a crossroads between accepting and denying this reality.

***

My story reached a peak in the conclusion to Leipzig, Germany. I found my song to sing and confirmed all six tools for navigating change. The only question remaining is what the hell happened after March 13th, 2020.

These last few chapters are my diary from the pandemic. While they only scratch the surface of 2020, I could not complete my story without highlighting some of my own experiences in that year like no other. As such, I divided this final section into introductory, concluding, and four "case study" chapters. Each highlights a notable event in the months from April through July 2020, episodes which capture the very essence of my life in the pandemic. Furthermore, they highlight many of my six ingredients for navigating change and demonstrate how these themes transcended my final undergraduate semester.

One of my favorite films leading up to March 13th, 2020 was the Russo Brothers' *Avengers: Infinity War*, a movie that perplexed me with the following question: *is destiny fixed or fluid?*

The pandemic ignited a series of debates over destiny, fate, and the damnable havoc this pestilence created all over the world. I've seen many argue that this period irrevocably changed our destinies by draining empty houses and inciting full streets that were never meant to be. My high school microbiology teacher always said I would experience a pandemic in my lifetime, and while the virus has certainly changed the lives of myself and everyone around me, I have an alternate view of fate in this chaotic time.

Perhaps our destinies were not altered, but rather always meant to encounter this bizarre chapter in human history. Just as those exit signs on the Pennsylvania Turnpike remained steadfast for my entire life, so too were we always destined to encounter and *endure* this unbelievable challenge.

My mind wanders back to those four pandemic stories as my family and I drive farther into New Jersey on this Saturday afternoon. They reaffirm my belief in our endurance and leave me, most importantly, with a profound sense of hope for the America I know.

ACCEPTANCE

Pandemic time is strange time. Life moves at light speed and a snail's pace. Internet connectivity increases while social interactions diminish. The virus spreads with haste though its symptoms appear slowly.

Even my dreams can't escape a godforsaken duality. They spiral into repetitive decay when some insistent buzz grows louder by my side. I crack both eyes open, roll over, and swat my phone off my nightstand. I only need one look down at the floor before retreating once again under the covers.

It's Thursday April 9th, 2020, and I'm almost one month into online college. Campus is a ghost town, nothing but deserted city blocks. My commute, in-person coursework, and social engagements are no more, flattened by a barrage of virtual classes, animated Senior Design group chats, and endless hours hunched over my thin black computer.

The clock reads 9:32 a.m.

Cheers to another day in the quarantine.

Both legs spill over my bed and drag me to the familiar perch in front of our coffeemaker. I leave the beans to brew, reenter my room in search of said computer, and unplug the charging cord. Its black metallic case stares me down as I confront a deflating fact: I still haven't heard anything about my English teaching applications. I was so sure of my potential for these programs after leaving Leipzig, but all feelings of good luck fade like distant memories as the timeline for acceptances passed me by weeks ago.

I return to the kitchen with my computer and pour scalding hot coffee into my trusty calculus-themed mug. Whiffs of steam twirl through the air as I enter the front porch and plop down on our green futon. Birds on the Japanese Maple tree greet me with their own songs to sing and lighten the mood before another fruitless search for closure.

Every morning routine is identical: cross my fingers, check the inbox, riffle through spam, recheck the inbox.

I open my computer for today's repetition, click the Chrome icon, and select my overused email bookmark. My inbox shows two unread messages and I wipe a thin layer of dust off the screen to clarify the fuzzy sender names. I delete the first email and focus on the second, haphazardly rubbing my eyes before reading the following subject line:

Herzlichen Glückwunsch: your 2020–21 USTA application

My heart rate skyrockets to a thousand beats per minute, daring my clammy fingers to inch the mouse closer to this unread message from Fulbright Austria. The birds, their songs, and the sunlight vanish as I squint to read the following text:

Dear Mr. Brock,

Fulbright Austria (Austrian-American Educational Commission) has coordinated the applications of US citizens for the Foreign Language Teaching Assistantship Program of the Austrian Federal Ministry of Education, Science and Research (BMBWF) since 1962, and as the program officer responsible for the management of this program, I am pleased to inform you that the BMBWF has notified Fulbright Austria that you have been selected to be a US teaching assistant (USTA) for the 2020–21 academic year. Herzlichen Glückwunsch!

I drop the computer on our futon and spring out of my seat. Streaks of sunlight envelop my body while Des opens the front door to shrieks and squeals.

"DES!!!" I scream, "I got it! I got Austria!!!"

"Oh my God, that's amazing! Congrats!" he shouts back before we embrace. His timing was nothing short of perfect. I run into the front yard, close my eyes, and pump my right fist into the air.

"Finally!" I exclaim, laughing to myself, "I really, finally got it."

Des joins me outside in the twinkling morning dew. I clasp my hands together and turn to him once again, beaming like a young kid consumed by overbearing excitement. Nothing seems more right in the world as the birds resume their chirps in the shining Japanese Maple.

If singing *Das Orchester* was the final ascent of some great mountain, then receiving this acceptance is like observing every shimmering view from its summit. Though I'm instantly hit by a flood of different memories in this moment of reflection, I drift back to one brief interaction before my departure to Germany.

I was sitting upstairs on the sixth floor of Temple's engineering building when two unfamiliar students asked me what I was doing. My red German binder was open on the table in front of me with notes and worksheets scattered all about.

"German," the one scoffed, "why would you waste your time studying that?"

"Well," I replied, "I enjoy learning this new language and want to teach English overseas."

He glances at the other and smirks. "You should have taken a coding course instead. Much better use of your time. I mean, don't they already speak English?"

I left that confrontation with even greater determination to defy the odds as an engineer teaching English in Europe.

Speak English to native German speakers. Sure, they might understand, but should native English speakers always hide behind their widely spoken language? The toxic mentality of "only English for English's sake" hinders cultural exchange and the potential for building new relationships. One need not completely master a second language, but a concerted effort to communicate in someone else's mother tongue builds bridges in this interconnected world. In my case, those bridges will soon span the Atlantic from the United States to Austria.

This acceptance was one of two that graced my email in April 2020, as I also received a US Fulbright English Teaching Assistantship in Germany one week after my Austrian notification. Though the possibility of returning to Germany was more than enticing, I accepted the US Teaching Assistantship in Austria for a slew of personal and logistical reasons. Most importantly, I took my chance on Austria because it, unlike Germany, was a new culture and part of the world I knew practically nothing about.

The equation introduced in Fall 2018 is finally complete. It was unfinished for quite some time after Leipzig and there's nothing like the finalized calculation shown below:

Hockey + Music + Physics + Dissent
+ Derry + Officiating
+ Mechanical Engineering + German
= Austria

Acceptance completes the arc in my fellowships journey and draws from my most important experiences since that 6th grade activities fair with Rinaldi. High school passions mixed with dissent and led to holistic international education in

Derry. The relationships from officiating then combined with dissent and my international interests to produce the necessary attitude for a leap of faith on German. Afterwards, I used a hefty dose of *Ohne Bedenken* to succeed in the *Musikstadt Leipzig* presentation and fellowship application process. It's hard to appreciate how many other science and engineering majors left their fields to teach English abroad, but I could not have been the first. More so am I confident to not be the last.

My pursuit of teaching overseas was by no means singular. It was only one of a million leaps of faith confirmed during the pandemic. My acceptance was among thousands of successful fellowship applications and is evidence of our collective potential in dire times. You, just like Ivy and my peers who took a chance on fellowships, jobs, or just getting through this strange period, can defy the odds and plot your own course through treacherous waters.

Let this be your final call to action. I know there must be something lurking inside, a thought which is both electrifying and terrifying at your core. You know its rewards, acknowledge the risks, and stand at a crossroads like the America I know.

What appeals to you like nothing else, that goal which sets itself above the rest?

Which of the six tools for change will help you navigate 10 percent situations and 90 percent possibilities?

What will it ultimately take for a gamble on your truest desires?

You are worth your leap of faith! Pave the path of your dreams and push yourself to that final finish line at the end of a long and prosperous journey. Even without precedent, you can absorb and embody the conviction needed to complete new tasks, become a better person, and make the future you want to see. There will be those willing to support your endeavors; all it takes is going out there and finding them.

While I began my journey to Austria on April 9th, 2020, all paths to a normal university graduation were never to be realized. Traditional academic celebrations vanished, leaving hardly a trace like all other events planned during the quarantine. Though I never completed a ceremonial walk through the streets of Philadelphia, I approached the final days of undergraduate study with a new tool offering hope for graduations in the year like no other: Zoom.

GRADUATION INTO THE UNKNOWN

May 2020 was a singular month. It was a transition point bridging the quarantine and first signs of a restless summer. Some days moved like molasses, sticky with anxiety about the future. Others were barren and empty after April showers failed to curtail the virus.

Some of my greatest excitement in those vacant May days came from spontaneous car rides around suburban Pennsylvania. I zipped under blossoming trees and sped through wafts of falling pollen, signs of rebirth that contrasted from an overarching feeling of death. The duality could not have been more pronounced and I kept my mind off the subject with the one thing I could do: keep on driving.

My family was at the center of my quarantine experiences. We laughed, cried, and persevered through long stretches of time at home. Our lives had forever changed after March 13th, 2020, but we trudged onward with the knowledge that togetherness is the most important blessing in the darkest of times. Every day tested our ability to live together peacefully, accomplish all personal obligations, and then abide by the natural goal of staying healthy. We squeaked shreds of normality out of an abnormal period, and while some life milestones were brutally interrupted in May 2020, not all succumbed to the virus' reign of terror. The pandemic challenged us to adapt, and we responded with my graduation into the unknown.

We agreed to hold our own graduation ceremony on May 8th at 5:00 p.m., one day after Temple's online commencement. From high school graduation on June 8th, 2016 to university commencement on May 8th, 2020, it seems that numerical pairings are a recurring theme in my life. My brother and I were born on the same day in different months, and the number eight became a defining aspect in my advancement from one educational pursuit to another.

Frank Sinatra's *September of My Years* album plays softly in my bedroom while I assemble my graduation attire on May 8th, 2020: white undershirt, cream-colored dress shirt, khaki pants, black belt. Sounds of preparation in the kitchen blend with Sinatra's prose as my mom spares no detail in planning today's festivities.

"Steve," she asks, "can you get the Prosecco?"

"Got it," echoes from somewhere down in the basement.

I recognize the thumps of my brother's footsteps through my closed bedroom door. "I'm going to do a special performance for everyone on Zoom."

"Oh yeah," responds my mom, "what kind? With your clarinet?"

"No," he likely grins, "something even better."

I can just imagine her expression.

"Now Des, nothing too crazy please."

"Hey don't worry, it won't be. I prooomise."

Whether he keeps his word is the real question of today's celebration.

I reach into the depths of my closet and procure a thin, auburn tie, one almost matching Temple's famous "cherry" color. Then comes my black graduation gown with a Temple "T" embroidered on the top left shoulder. I throw it over my head, pat down the sides, and zipper up the front two pieces. Adorning the hood causes me trouble and I finally make it presentable after watching a few instructional videos on my phone. The cap and tassel then complete my outfit, the icing on top of this graduation cake. I shuffle over to my large circular mirror as *September of My Years* transitions to a different Sinatra album.

"I'm good to go, it's almost five," I call out, now sitting on my bed. "How we doing?"

"One minute!" declares my mom. "Let me get the Zoom ready and then we'll start."

I lay back onto my bed and smile as defining moments from the last four years drift in and out of my consciousness, evoking joy and pain, success and failure. These memories embody my university experiences but strike me with an unexpected question: What is it exactly that made the last four years so memorable? My classes, study abroad? Perhaps the people?

Adults always reminded me to treasure college dearly when I was a child. They said you won't know how fast it'll go, enjoy every minute, best years of my life, wish I could go back. All of these statements share a sense of longing, not necessarily regret, but the desire to reach out and touch something that's no longer there to grasp. Their time as university students is long gone, so why do they keep wishing?

I believe it is quite common to yearn for the "good ole' days," a return to memories that depict better times than the present. High school and college very well may have been some of the best years in my life, but I have no intent to live with complete jealousy of the past.

If I learned one thing from Joss Whedon's *Avengers: Age of Ultron*, then it's that there's beauty to be found in the limits of our existence. This notion transcends almost all chapters in my life, from music to hockey to adventures overseas. I treasure the individual colors in my self-portrait because they confine themselves within the frame. It is from the limitations of my experiences, and the knowledge that my time on this Mother Earth is finite, that I find purpose to enjoy and make the best out of every opportunity I encounter.

The dominoes of life tip in sequence and trade momentum from one story to another. My own table of contents is filled with the dominoes of the past ten years or so, and the ones from Temple have finally taken their place on the table. I completely agree with adults' admiration of the past, but I'm not reaching back forever. My memories, whether the tears of my breakdown or full glasses of *Gose* and Guinness, will be my drive to persist beyond this graduation, through the summer, and as an American in Austria.

***

"Alright, ready!"

I spring off the bed and pat down my gown one last time. A few steps forward lead me out of my room and into the spotlight.

My bedroom door opens to the basement of the *Moritzbastei*. The sun sneaks through several windows like the stained glass in Temple's Performing Arts Center and sets a mood in contrast from the performance of Lo Presti's *Elegy*. Walnut-colored flooring is the red carpet to a fictional microphone like the real ones I played beside in the Hershey Theater and Lodge at PMEA All-State Band. My mom stands at the ready with a cherry-colored scarf and earrings. To her left lies our kitchen table with candles, fancy glasses, and a sweating bottle of Prosecco. My dad and brother wait near the entrance to our living room.

I spot my mom's computer resting on the countertop with an active Zoom call. I see nothing but smiles and the tiny faces of extended family and friends on the screen as I stride across the kitchen and enter our living room. My brother pulls out his phone and begins playing Elgar's *Pomp and Circumstance*, a classic at American graduations. I proceed to the kitchen table after completing two laps around the living room.

"Now it's time for the official diploma presentation!" announces my mom.

She lifts up her own Temple University diploma out from under a placemat. Mine would not arrive for another several weeks, and as always, she's prepared for a unique situation. It reads "Kimberly Schuler for her Masters of Science in Occupational Health and Safety," the degree she also earned from Temple's College of Engineering in the early 1990's.

"Now, Adam Nicholas Brock," she begins, raising the diploma to chest level. "I would like to use the powers invested in me as a former Temple graduate to present you today with this diploma for your accomplishments at Temple University."

She hands over the frame and slightly shifts position to address both me and the virtual audience of family and friends.

"Let us now welcome one of Temple's newest graduates from the Class of 2020!!"

Applause erupts from the Zoom call as I symbolically shift the tassel on my cap from right to left. I put the diploma down and lean to hug my mom and fellow alumnus.

"Congratulations buddy," she whispers as we embrace.

Pomp and Circumstance suddenly halts to my brother's procurement of every fourth grader's favorite instrument in the Colonial School District: a plastic recorder.

"Adam, listen, I learned how to play this today!"

Des begins what can only be the Elgar. His recorder is too small to hit the lowest note in the main theme but this "surprise" is even better than I expected. My dad takes out his phone and snaps some pictures, first of me and my mom and then me with Des on the recorder. I still look through those photos from time to time and reminisce over some of life's simplest moments.

"How 'bout we start showing some respect for the people on Zoom?" interjects a ballsy Rinaldi from the computer. He's never one to waste any opportunity for drama.

"You'll be muted before you know it," I fire back.

He's joined by Ivy, our friend Emma from engineering, and all the members of our immediate family. We congratulate Ivy and Emma for graduating before more chatter from Rinaldi and loud barks from Aunt Anita's dog Butkus upset her and Cousin Gia. Grandmom Janice tries to console them both while Uncle John asks if I'll be looking to date anyone overseas. I'll have to get back to him about that one.

Long-time family friends Ki Soo, KJ, and Michaela ask about our plans after graduation before my grandfather Rich reminds us that, in fact, we're not finished celebrating.

"How about a cheers?" he bellows into the chat. "Looks like you guys haven't opened that Prosecco."

"Hey, he's right, we forgot about the toast," responds my dad.

"Everyone grab a drink, we'll do one virtually."

Faces disappear as my relatives and friends go gather their favorite beverages, be it my grandfather's blackberry brandy or classic American beers for my aunt and uncle. We collect glasses from the kitchen table and pop open the Prosecco.

My family is my backbone. All those hockey games, music concerts, years at Temple, and everything in between came from their willingness to accept and support my endeavors. When the time then arrived for my leap of faith on Leipzig, all they needed was a plan and purpose. Now and then I'm asked how it was possible to do so many different activities during high school and as a commuter in college. Was it some special power, maybe a secret weapon or magic potion? Sometimes the toughest questions have the simplest answers and this case is no different.

My superpower is no secret: it's my family.

Our relationships and attitudes were already critical before March 13th, 2020 and proved themselves even more essential in fostering good spirits during the pandemic. My acceptance to Austria was a highlight of the quarantine for good reason, but it was in the little things and our everyday perseverance that gave me hope in a sea of darkness. The virus removed our commutes, brought my brother home from school, and even cancelled a normal graduation; however, it did not take away family dinners, moonlit walks around our neighborhood, and time spent by a wood-burning stove in our basement which still, to this day, make us who we are.

This celebration was something I both never expected and would do again without hesitation. Thankfully, my

Zoom graduation was not the only event that adapted to the early pandemic. There were other yearly pilgrimages that my friends and I would soon complete, ones which brought us a sense of normality in the great state of Pennsylvania.

"Adam, are you ready?" questions an impatient voice.

Looks like we're not yet done with the toast. Des apparently can't hold back his itch for Prosecco, and while I would normally make him sweat for it, the man did bring out his recorder. Cheers to that alone!

I ready myself in front of the computer as friends and relatives assemble their drinks. It's impossible to hold back a grin while raising my glass to our audience.

"On the count of three," begins my mom.

"Alright everybody, now one, two..."

THE PENNSYLVANIA GRAND CANYON

Time to load the supplies. Fishing gear, boots, tackle, bait. Hey, get both coolers, can't forget the venison. Alcohol, hmm, let's get it in Wellsboro. Gonna surprise the boys with this blowtorch, damn that's hot. Camping chair, hammock...can't forget the hammock.

More gas? Ehh, tank's almost full, can fill 'er up again in Williamsport. Got the grill for some fine breakfasts, will get seasoning at Tops. Hey, where's the machete? Ah, left it down in Maryland. Good thing we got the axe.

Hope these city boys are ready for 'nother long trip.

Bo Flint pauses after slamming the tailgate on his pickup truck. He wipes the sweat off his brow, climbs on up into the driver seat of Gertrude, his trusty gray Ford F150, and revs the engine. Like the city of Leipzig, Bo is a man of many names and talents. He is also the central figure in another yearly pilgrimage to the Pennsylvania Grand Canyon.

Also known as the Pine Creek Gorge, the Canyon stretches for forty-seven miles within Tioga, Clinton, and Lycoming counties. It bustles with life along Pennsylvania's northern border and shows few signs of the damage once endured from destructive logging practices.

Bo picks me up in early June 2020 for what is now the fourth installment of our annual camping trip. Started on nothing more than a whim back in high school, yearly visits to the Pennsylvania Grand Canyon are now part of my identity with the boys back home.

We're joined by twins, Matt and Jim, two sides of the Gatta family coin. They're a pair of trolls, those two, always jostling for another step up on ole' Bo and me. Though they're riding separately on the roughly four-hour drive to Wellsboro, the largest town near the Canyon, there's one feeling we all share on the trip from Philadelphia.

The Canyon is calling.

I can hardly wait to see Pine Creek slithering its way between outlooks scattered along the Canyon's jagged cliffs. Indecisive clouds will likely taunt us for the entire weekend, making unexpected appearances to only vanish as quickly as they came. I imagine how sparkles off the water might entertain the elevated observer while we, traveling on foot through heat and humidity along the riverbank, will only wonder how they look from above.

Bo blasts a Jimmy Buffett playlist as we begin the long trip north on Interstate 476. I lean out the passenger window and sigh, awaiting what is likely my last trip to Wellsboro for a long time coming. With university graduations behind us and only three months until my departure to Austria, this year's adventure with the boys may very well be my last. My journeys to the Canyon, like all experiences at Temple, are finite in number. While I'm certainly determined to make the most out of our upcoming excursion, I have no idea that this trip to Canyon country will reunite us with a blast from our past.

We usually set up in Colton Point State Park but decide to find a new campground for this year's adventure. Several hours pass before we, the so-called "Canyon Men," finally arrive at a tucked-away campsite near Tiadaghton State Forest. Bo eyed up this location for the wild trout supposedly running along Slate Run Creek while the Gatta boys and I were fond of Tiadaghton's towering pine trees and seclusion.

Campsite construction is nothing new to us "city boys" and we unload our supplies under the retreating sun. Pine needles cushion our feet as the tent rises on a slightly slanted hillside, the hammock finds its place between two trees, and the firewood seeks false refuge in a makeshift firepit. Bo then arrives with what brings a smile to all of our faces: a crisp, cool 30-rack.

He cracks the first beer beside our campfire as we descend into darkness. The Canyon slowly ladles an opaque soup over our campsite, a blackness so thick and dense that I lose sight of both hands when extending them in front of my body. That first beer is followed by a second, and with the second comes a third, and after the fourth begins what I can only describe as the usual shit.

Matt takes two swigs from a half-filled sweet tea bottle.

"Pops, how ya feelin' about the Johnny Doolittle?"

I'm known as an old man in many of my social circles and the Canyon Men are no exception. Johnny Doolitte derives from the ubiquitous John Daly, a mixed drink made of lemonade, iced tea, and vodka. It first morphed into James Doley, then John Dotley, John Doolity, and finally, Johnny Doolittle.

"C'mon, take another swig of the Johnny D's."

"Nah Donnie, you know this old man ain't what he used to be," I chirp back. Donnie, close enough to Matt. "These old bones can't take no more of that Doolittle."

Even at normal speaking volume it is fair to say campers on the other side of the canyon can probably hear me barking into the night. How I don't blow out my own eardrums is as great a question for me as for the Canyon Men. Then again, if you think I'm loud, just listen to my father.

"Ah, leave it to the old timer to chicken out of a good time. I simply can't believe it," chimes a feisty Jim. He can't leave all the chatter to his brother.

"Well guys," contributes a sentimental Bo while staring intently into the flames, "I think we really lucked out with this camp site."

He holds the group axe in one hand and a cup of Johnny D's in the other. That's all it takes for the fun to begin.

"Got that one right, Goobie old pal."

"Hey Cogsy, pass me another cold one would ya?"

"Come on Mr. Duck, I know you want another swig of the sweet JD's. Don't fight it."

Goobie, Cogsy, Mr. Duck. A man of many names indeed.

I occasionally toss another pine branch into the insatiable pit as we continue on with our banter. Each piece of fuel leaves its mark in the leaping flames, a normal occurrence in times that are anything but. Our fireside bullshit isn't the only thing wracking my brain, and as the boys keep slugging back their liquid courage, I shift away from our conversation with a memory from my immediate past.

The shade offers cooling refreshment on an otherwise sweltering day in late May 2020. My mom and I sit in chairs on our back patio and recline under the giant Sycamore tree which rules the backyard. We rest in nearly identical spots to our German conversation with my dad from nearly one and a half years ago. Though a new life in Central Europe draws closer by the day, my most immediate focus is limited to the upcoming Canyon trip. So too are the thoughts of my mom.

"So," she says, looking up from a Sudoku book on her lap, "who's committed for next weekend?"

"Just me, Bo, and the Gattas," I reply. "Could be more but I suspect it's just the four of us."

She peers down at a new puzzle.

"I remember when you all were in preschool together."

I look over swiftly, head cocked to one side.

"Were we actually?"

"Yep, same class over at a school in Chestnut Hill. Teacher said it was so great to watch you guys build towers and play sports with one another. Probably some of your earliest friendships before kindergarten."

I immediately snap back to the campfire with that Sudoku book stapled into my subconscious. Those pre-k memories still elude me, but I can distinctly recall the four of us playing sports together, whether that was ice hockey for Bo and me or soccer for the three of them. We grew more distant as the years went on and our paths eventually diverged in late elementary and middle school. Now, over a decade after one passion for athletics brought us together in preschool, the Canyon men reunite with another common interest: exploring our backyard in Pennsylvania.

"Hey now boys," I vocalize while sipping some loose foam from my beer, "want to know something interesting my mom recently told me?"

"Of course Pops," pipes up Jim. "Give us the deets."

"I don't know how much you guys remember from preschool, but we were apparently all good friends in the same class. Played sports and shit with one another. Imagine coming back together a few years ago after all that time, just the four of us."

Mr. Duck is the first to chime in.

"Well I'll say. Makes sense from the little I remember, but damn, can't believe it goes back that far."

"Yeah," acknowledges Donnie. "Look where we've come, that's wild."

The conversation pauses, briefly replaced by crackling logs and branches in front of us.

"Alright," I chirp up, "pass me the Doolittle. It's time."

"That a guy Pops!"

I take a huge swig of the super-sweet drink and gaze around at my fellow Canyon Men.

This fourth journey to the Canyon completes the arc of our relationships since elementary school. With nothing more than the forest, our fire, and cans of cool refreshment, the boys and I were able to come together and escape the maddening pandemic if only for a weekend. While passions for music and hockey brought me together with Luke and Rinaldi, I solidified old bonds with the Canyon Men through interests in the outdoors.

It's no secret between the four of us that we may not share the same values and beliefs in this time of full streets. Although our trip to the Canyon coincides with increasing restlessness in the America I know, such tension is irrelevant to friends who gather for reasons greater than their own personal biases. This retreat in Tiadaghton State Forest supports my hope for the future that we, as Americans, can overcome our differences in the pandemic with the strength of everything that unites us. My family first proved its determination to come together with a nontraditional graduation, and the baton then fell easily into the hands of four Canyon Men in the Pennsylvania Grand Canyon.

The ultimate test of America's ability to bridge its divides followed this Canyon trip in the midst of the pandemic summer. I witnessed a crisis which tempted the Americans I know with a chance for unity at the highest stakes possible. This summer adventure sent me in the opposite direction from Wellsboro, Pennsylvania, to my second home on the eastern seaboard. I hope you're ready for some warmer weather because I'm traveling south to a beach town treasured by Brocks for generations.

Next stop: Cape May, New Jersey.

JULY 17TH, 2020

Beach days are lazy days. I wake with a yawn and stretch my back. The beaches of Cape May, New Jersey prepare for slumber after another sweltering mid-summer afternoon. Umbrellas sway in a steady breeze and cast cooling shadows over the occasional beach chair. I rub my eyes, roll over on my family's beach blanket, and check my phone.

The digital clock reads nearly 6:00 p.m. on July 17th, 2020. Wispy clouds dot the sky while crashing waves compete with the incessant screaming of seagulls for supremacy over my ears. The retreating sun elongates every ray and bends them over each footprint in the sand. Despite all signs to the contrary, this late afternoon will test the very souls of the Americans I know.

I set my phone back down without a care in the world and snuggle into my beach chair. My toes dig deep into the coarse sand beside our blanket as I open my tattered copy of Claudio Magris' *Danube*. The pandemic has interrupted many traditions but no virus will prevent my summer reading in Cape May.

Magris' prose immediately kidnaps my attention. He and I disappear into dreams of Central Europe, a part of the world I will soon embrace upon arriving in Austria. Magris snatches me from the New Jersey coast and transports us far from the summer of empty houses and full streets. We wander along the Danube from southern Germany to the Black Sea, encountering sunsets like the one which graced my high school graduation. Magris charms me with history, poetry, and walks along the soft embankments of Europe's second longest river. He extracts my excitement and apprehension regarding the upcoming move to Austria, taunting the very journey I've taken since the beginning of college.

The bridges built over these last four years have already sent me quite a distance, from the streets of Philadelphia to the Northern Irish coast, from Liberty University to the basement in Leipzig's *Moritzbastei*. Now, with my departure just two months away, Magris confronts me with my future. The start of my English teaching position in Austria draws nearer by the day, and although the pandemic continues ranging across the globe, there are no signs of cancellation or any change in plans. My compass points increasingly eastward toward Europe, but on July 17th, 2020, there is still much to do on the beaches of Cape May, New Jersey.

Piercing screams tear me away from my book. I shake my head and plug both ears, but there's no escaping this high-pitched shrill. Images of the Danube and Austria fall out of view as I sit up in my chair and turn to face the water.

Desperate shrieks disturb our family blanket once again and slowly trail off to a whimper. I stand up, raise my hand to block out the sun, and see the familiar umbrellas, chairs, and sandcastles on Cape May's Perry Street Beach. I look past empty lifeguard stands in pursuit of the noise. The shrills repeat and I take a few steps closer to the water.

The ocean churns and swells under the setting sun. Impatient waves slam the shoreline, shooting wafts of foam into the air. Clumps of seaweed and stray logs litter the water's surface and perform an indecisive dance among the swirling currents.

Rainbows form for mere seconds above the chaotic shoreline, though they're no comfort alongside those guttural shouts.

I move closer to the water's edge and stand beside the wooden lifeguard boat while conducting a sweep of the coastline. Other beachgoers rise from their blankets and join me, their hands also raised to block out the retreating sun.

Mine drop at the first sign of trouble. I look far beyond the water's edge and spot five young kids bobbing in the ocean. They cling to neon-colored surfboards as the sea continues its battle with the shore. Their one source of comfort drags them farther from safety, to a horizon growing darker by the second.

There are three girls and two boys. Most share a mid-summer tan. They scream once again, their high-pitched voices cresting above the perpetual drum of pounding waves and hungry seagulls. Their position among ocean debris yields an unsettling conclusion: they're caught in the rip.

Rip currents are some of the most dangerous hazards along New Jersey beaches. Identifiable by light, foamy water and often cluttered with sticks and seaweed, they are a quick one-way ticket out to sea.

The people of Perry Street Beach swarm the coastline like a flock of seagulls as my mom and dad join me by the lifeguard boat. We are all that stands between those kids' return to safety and a rip current ready to suck them out into a merciless ocean.

I take a step back as the crowd grows exponentially and look around at this group of fellow Americans.

I see Americans of all colors. Black, white, every shade in between. Some are old, others young.

I see American men and women. Tall and thin, short and heavy, every dimension in between. Some carry kids, others tattoos and piercings.

I see Americans of various identities. Left and liberal, right and conservative, every viewpoint in between. Some take pride in their beliefs, others in their silence.

Most importantly, I see the Americans I know spring into action at the sight of those stranded kids. They sprint to the water's edge as one group to serve something greater than themselves. Over two dozen adult swimmers charge into the waves when a man approaches me by the lifeguard boat.

"Let's get this thing in the water!"

His face is stern, mouth open, forehead clenched. He yanks one side of the boat before I can even respond.

"Where are the oars?!" he shouts.

"Lifeguards packed them into a box near the promenade," I reply. "Pretty sure it's locked up after hours."

"Fuck!" he yells, bringing his hands to his face before bolting directly into the water.

I stand in awe of these Americans before running behind them and entering to waist level. I pursue the others as they dive through the waves, pounded by every new crash and the ever-present pull of the rip. Swimmers of all shapes, talents, and speeds hastily pursue their singular objective, clawing through each challenge with renewed strength in pursuit of those stranded children. They dash out into the ocean without reservation, without fear that one American may suffer in the rescue of another. The man from the lifeguard boat splashes behind the front of the crowd as they swim head-first through waves and approach those neon surfboards.

The Americans I know reach the desperate kids by the time my parents and I are chest deep. They grab ahold of the surfboards and begin a round trip to the shoreline. Each child glues themselves to the Americans and their boards as the rescuers plow through stubborn water. The children's screams are soon drowned out by the sirens of emergency lifeguards, fire trucks, and medical staff arriving on scene. The Americans break the rip and exit the water with surfboards and children at their sides.

Every child lands in the arms of a parent or emergency responder, finally free from the treacherous surf. Their return to shore draws even more people and attention to the Perry Street Beach. I follow the rescuers and stand at the ocean's edge. Water drips off my body into the footprints of the Americans I know as they retreat into the giant crowd of onlookers.

Black and white, tall and small, left and right. The swimmers disband as quickly as they came and return to blankets and the open arms of friends and family. I watch this sea of Americans disappear, lost to an ocean of our peers.

***

The year like no other brought a decades' worth of change to the America I know. Between the quarantine, full streets, and an ever-changing pandemic, my home for over twenty years seemed to be caving in on itself.

Today's events proved my fears unfounded. Beach days are only lazy until a call to action, and as I silently observe those Americans vanishing into the crowds of Cape May, I receive an answer to a question posed long ago in the restless summer.

On July 17th, 2020, I saw Americans prove the America I know still exists. Despite fears of contracting the virus, toxic political division, life-threatening rip currents, and the fact that these children remained strangers after their rescue, the people of Cape May proved their ability to unite in the most dire circumstances. Rather than conforming to the confrontation and bitterness on America's full streets, those rescuers of all colors, shapes, and beliefs chose to dive headfirst into a rip current. They demonstrated how the forces of division, just like some of the superficial social, political, and religious affiliations used to rip Americans apart, are only as powerful as they are allowed to be.

Those Americans are a message of unity in fractured times. Lo Presti composed one man an elegy, so I wrote them a homage. They are my hope for the future, the greatest weapons against threats of separation and disunion. If they could choose a path of selflessness and cooperation, then there's no reason why you or I cannot follow suit in other facets of life.

I walked back to our family blanket and left the beach with my parents after those Americans disappeared among the crowd. As I pedaled my bike away from the shoreline and heard waves crashing far off in the distance, my mind still contemplated the extraordinary actions of ordinary people on the Perry Street Beach.

I was once so concerned with March 13th, 2020. It was a transitional day, my one-way ticket between two separate lives. I now posit that the summer of empty houses and full streets be remembered for a different date, one which confirmed my hope for the America I know.

Let the date of July 17th, 2020 be the day of America's awakening, the realization that we, as Americans, can choose to be united.

GRAZ

I gaze out from the back left passenger seat in my mom's SUV. Her car glides over unfamiliar bumps on the New Jersey Turnpike as I stare out at the exit signs. They float by like dandelions in the wind:

Perth Amboy, Garden State Parkway, Rahway, Staten Island, Newark Airport

Every off-ramp reveals a new set of signs with missing spots of paint. When I was younger, I would eagerly wait for the exits, wondering if today might be the day when they would no longer abide by the usual names and numbers. I was biding my time for that inevitable surprise, a rush of excitement from some variation in routine commutes with my mom.

Different signs, renamed exits, perhaps a whole new turnpike? Everything finally changed, and the wait was surely worth it.

My brother sits to my right, his chaotic head of hair tamed into gelled waves of brown, while my dad sits shotgun and mom in the driver's seat. Suitcases bounce around the trunk in unison with the occasional change in road material. A light gray sky sketches sentimental clouds on the car's reflective exterior as we approach Terminal B at Newark Liberty International Airport.

Welcome back to September 2020. It's over a full year since *Das Orchester* filled the airwaves in Leipzig's *Moritzbastei* and my time in the America I know has come to an end. My position as an English teaching assistant begins in two weeks, an experience I have pursued since November 2018 but never believed would actually happen. A full year abroad, in the flesh. Impossible.

This September echoes May 2020, a transition point between two phases of life. We pull up into the short-term parking area and stop under the ticker for Austrian Airlines. My flight to Vienna and one night in a Viennese apartment lie ahead before the final leg in my journey: a three-hour train ride to Graz, Austria.

I graduated into the unknown and now am flying into it. Despite all the packing and planning, this next chapter in my life only became real when I was preparing to leave for Newark in our shared family bathroom.

I walked up to the sink and pulled my electric toothbrush off the charging station. A soft morning light illuminated sections of pink wallpaper as I applied a dollop of blue toothpaste, wet the brush head under the sink faucet, and began the electric motor. I lifted the toothbrush and eyed myself in the bathroom mirror, ready for one last morning cleaning. I looked down at the spinning wad of toothpaste, gazed back into my reflection, and started sobbing.

Blue globs mixed with a salty waterfall in the slanted bathroom sink until tears were all that remained. Unable to reach for more toothpaste, I set down the toothbrush and peeked up at the mirror. My gaze returned a bright-red face as I stood there motionless. I was the conductor of that liquid waterfall with a toothbrush as my baton. This final morning tradition, a consistent habit I learned from my parents nearly two decades ago, marked the end of an era. No full suitcase or boarding pass could ever be more surreal than one final teeth cleaning in our pink bathroom. All it took was toothpaste, my reflection, and the mirror I'd been using for my entire life.

The face I stared into was reminiscent of the one I saw in early high school. It was once the face of a young clarinetist pursuing physics with his arms wide open for the "traditional" college experience. Four years later, it's the face of an Austrian fellowship recipient preparing to go abroad and teach English during a pandemic. After wiping my nose and pausing to breathe, I looked back at the mirror with my leaps of faith in mind. Then I reapplied more toothpaste, cleaned those teeth to a sparkling finish, and packed my toothbrush for one last time.

I have no intention of turning back now. Every experience since that sixth grade activities fair, my entire journey through the past eleven years, had been preparing me for a new life in Graz. The time had come to move forward, to find the 90 percent response to my 10 percent situation in Austria, whatever it will be.

The one critical detail I've often excluded from my 10 percent is the composition of this memoir. I stared down at my spinning toothbrush with a majority of these chapters already drafted, and just as my teaching abilities prepared for their first foreign test in Austria, so too did the completion of this project depend on my new life and future experiences in Central Europe.

The path to writing this final chapter had as many twists and turns as my journey to that eventful teeth cleaning. One of my favorite questions from the publication journey was as follows:

Adam, is it not a little selfish to write a memoir when you're so young? What could you possibly write about?

I still laugh at the first idea that came to mind: the golden fish jumps over the silver pond. This seemingly simple construction was quite complex in my mind as a first grader. It comes from one of the many homework assignments during those early years when writing sentences, forget books, was life's greatest challenge. My parents can tell stories about how frustrated I became when putting words next to one another; how my face would swell like a cherry at the start of a long journey to ten full sentences. For all I know, it was as red as my face with that toothbrush.

I will always remember this particular sentence because I based it off of something I heard a few days before. I suppose that makes me a cheater in first grade, but I doubt my elementary school teacher would hold a grudge against me now.

What could I possibly write about?

Well, at least there's the golden fish.

I may never compose a symphony, but this book is the closest I've come thus far. It is the continuation of all those journals from Derry, my fellowship applications to Germany and Austria, and the leap of faith I took on writing during the year like no other.

What is most frustrating about that publication question is its glaring assumption: no young adult has anything personal to write about.

I oppose suggestions that life is only describable by older authors. Age provides diversity and wealth of experience, but every person, young or old, collects stories during their existence on this Earth. We all undergo incredible growth and self-discovery in the journey through young adulthood and that is exactly what I've described in my memoir.

Rather than directly equating intelligence and writing ability with age, I prefer subscribing to Galileo in his *Letter to the Grand Duchess Christina of Tuscany, 1615:* "those truths which we know are very few in comparison with those which we do not." Just as the America I know must embrace the quest to realize its founding ideals, we all must recognize the limitations of our knowledge and respect Galileo's unknown truths.

Storytelling is the key to discovering everything we have left to learn and recording the human experience. Like physics and German, it is a language that brings people together. Storytelling solves the mystery of ourselves and everyone around us and draws inspiration and strength from all different aspects of life and everything that makes us whole.

I decided to pursue Galileo's unknown truths by writing. My story is a color wheel of bathroom mirror reflections, the tale of one man who followed his passions to dissent and holistic education in Europe. From there, the path forward required a combination of relationships, attitude, and *Ohne Bedenken* to find his song to sing. My personal and professional development in Austria, the next phase of life beyond our pink family bathroom, will greatly hinge on my lessons from the last several years and the hope extracted from the summer of empty houses and full streets.

This is my coming-of-age story and I chose to tell it. Composing my memoir helped wrap up many loose ends from my journey to Austria but this is by no means the end of my reflection. I'm hardly finished deciphering my own past and ask that you start digging into yours, travelling down the long path to discover all that constitutes your being, the glue of your identity.

You have a story to share. We've all lived through our own books and undergone periods of success and failure, triumph and loss. Whether black or white, tall or small, and left or right, the world will always have something to learn from your experiences and no tale is too short to tell. Maybe you're not a writer, and that's alright. Your story, whether a picture to paint, song to sing, or book to publish, is buried deep inside of you and waits like a dam about to burst. Realizing your potential as a storyteller will bring us one step closer to finding Galileo's unknown truths and, in the end, help us take our leaps of faith on the future.

If you don't take my word for it, then think back to Balmages' pre-concert speech. Whether you'll be a new author or the next principal horn of the Chicago Symphony, "you need to decide if it's going to be you."

My arrival to Terminal B starts another waterfall of comparable size to those mirror reflections and first grade sentence constructions. I have no toothbrush baton, but that won't stop the tears. My family and I drop my luggage on the sidewalk after what must have been the biggest embrace of my life. They know, as I now do, that today's face in the mirror will not be my last. I will return, and my next reflection will be of an American in Graz.

I wave both hands when they reenter my mom's SUV. We lock eyes, smile, and wave one last time as they slowly pull away from the sidewalk. I pause for a few seconds and soak in the late afternoon sun, wondering what new exits they'll encounter on the long ride home.

I lug a hefty suitcase into the terminal before walking back outside and retrieving my iPod with the rest of my luggage. I put headphones in both ears, press the "shuffle" button, and smile at the first selection. It's the recording of Maslanka's *Requiem* from 2016 PMEA All-States, the same song his *Program Note* describes for individuals experiencing changes in their lives.

The newest change in my life, and the beginning of a long journey, wait just one entrance away. I look once more at the sun, turn back to Terminal B, and stride forward with my clarinet case in one hand and officiating gear in the other. I readjust my headphones after the sliding doors close swiftly behind me.

ACKNOWLEDGMENTS

Writing is a communal process and I want to sincerely thank my family, friends, colleagues, all the characters, and everyone else in the *My Song to Sing* community. You are the spine of this book and behind every page, story, and chapter.

Many thanks to all the Beta Readers who spent countless hours reviewing early drafts and providing feedback. *My Song to Sing* benefited greatly from your input and I could have never completed this memoir without you.

Chirag Agarwal, Brian Balmages, Connor Berry, Dr. Gudrun Boch, Desmond Brock, Kimberly Brock, KJ Burkhauser, Ivy Nuo Chen, Monika Clark, Mike Delfin, Carole-Anne Ferguson, Nadja Halsegger, Tom Heinich, Rebecca Karpen, Emma Krampe, Jim Gatta, Matt Gatta, Dr. Barbara Gorka, Fiona Hickel, Dr. Shannon Kitelinger, Dr. Patricia Melzer, Brian Murphy, Sean Mullan, Annelise Myers, Martina Pichler, Jasmin Ramsbacher, Chris Rinaldi, Eric Scheidly, Luke Simons, Nathan Snyder, Dr. Suzanne Willever, Barbara Wrana, Dr. Ralph Young, and David Zimmer.

I would also like to thank Paige Buxbaum, Ilia Epifanov, and Eric Koester for facilitating this memoir's creation along with everyone who preordered *My Song to Sing*. I am forever grateful for your interest, support, and encouragement through all steps of the writing process.

Chirag Agarwal, Gabriel Altopp, Ray Banas, Ernestine Garnett-Banas, David Bartole, Stephanie Beard, Connor Berry, Andrew Bertolazzi II, Adiba Bhuiyan, Julia Brandstätter, Desmond Brock, Janice Brock, Kimberly Brock, Steven Brock, Dr. Gudrun Boch, Rob Bolz, Ki Soo Burkhauser, KJ Burkhauser, Michaela Burkhauser, Carmen Busara, Steven Capriotti, Samantha Carpenter, John Casey, Ashley Cavuto, Ivy Nuo Chen, Monika Clark, Josephine Content, Kelly Coons, Garret Corr, Renee Darcy, Mike D'Argenio, Bruno D'Avella, Charlie Dawes, Mike Delfin, Katherine Denning, Tess Deutermann, Joe DiFeo, Susan Dolan, Jack Dunphy, Alexandria Dunphy-Russo, Hannah Eckman, JJ Eisenlohr, Colin Fagan, Carole-Anne Ferguson, Monty Ferguson, Stu Fishman, Lynda Fiuza, Bruce Flint, Stephen Frick, Amanda Galczyk, Eric Garman, Jim Gatta, Matt Gatta, Jason Getchell, Daniel Giusti, Patrick Hanrahan, Eva Harant, Fiona Hickel, Monika Holzer, Brian Isely, Sabrina Jastram, Daniel Jovin, Chimere Kanu, Rebecca Karpen, Gurmeet Kaur, Gillian Kehs, Alyssa Kenney, Devin Kenny, Connor Kissane, Eric Koester, Jezreel Konstantinos, Emma Krampe, Jesse Krensel, Dr. Karin Kronabitter, Lawrence Kruglyak, Kirk Kumfert, Julie Lee, Anna Lenaker, Maria Lichtenegger, Sophie Lyu, Elisabeth Mairhofer, Christopher Manero, Jason Mensch, Irina Missethan, Karl Moehlmann, Justin Morman, Sean Mullan, Brian Murphy, Annelise Myers, Eunice Nam, Susha Nataraj, Karin Nutz, Justin Oakes, Sean O'Brien, Samantha Panich, Vera Paulla, Juliann Pearl, Owen Pearl, Michael Pettis, Martina Pichler, Gabe Preston, Michaela Primig, Ryan Probasco, Colleen Purdy, Jayci Reagan, Matt Refford, Dr. Laura Riggio, Chris Rinaldi, Thomas Russell, Ben Ryherd, Jack Sanders, Samantha Schafer, Leah Schick, Gavin Schmitt, Tricia Schmitt, Richard Schuler, Anita Sears, Gia Sears, John

Sears, Sonja Sengl, Elizabeth Shaloka, Lina Shi, Luke Simons, Aaron Skarzenski, Jake Smedley, Alexa Smith, Carly Smith, Nathan Snyder, Karin Strohmeier, Elke Stückler, Devon Taormina, Paul Thomas, Peter Troy, Gregory Van Buskirk, Gordon Walbert, Birgit Walzl, Birgit Winkler, Dr. Herbert Woi, Matt Wrightson, Sophia Yoo, Dr. Ralph Young, and David Zimmer.

I owe my interest in reading and writing to a great many authors and want to recognize them and some of my favorite books: Claudio Magris' *Danube: A Sentimental Journey from the Source to the Black Sea*, Ralph Young's *Dissent: The History of an American Idea*, Tyler Bamford's *Forging the Grand Alliance: The British and American Armies, 1917-1941*, William Manchester's *Goodbye, Darkness: A Memoir of the Pacific War*, Viktor Frankl's *Man's Search for Meaning*, Herman Melville's *Moby-Dick*, Sir Arthur Conan Doyle's *The Complete Sherlock Holmes*, Barbara Tuchman's *The Guns of August* and *The Proud Tower: A Portrait of the World Before the War, 1890-1914*, and Tim O'Brien's *The Things They Carried*.

Last but not least, I'd like to thank you, dear reader. I sincerely appreciate your interest in my memoir and would be happy to discuss *My Song to Sing* on Instagram. You can follow me at @adambrock_author. Keep reading and cheers to your next book!

APPENDIX

AUTHOR'S NOTE

Seeger, Pete. *Little Boxes*. Album: *Headlines and Footnotes: A Collection of Topical Songs*. 1999, originally recorded in 1963. Essex Music. Smithsonian Folkways Recordings. Streamed on Spotify.

HIGH SCHOOL

Bourne, Randolph. *The State*. 1918. Randolph Silliman Bourne papers; Box 7; Rare Book and Manuscript Library, Columbia University Library.

De Meij, Johan. "Symphony No. 1 The Lord of the Rings." Last modified 2021. Accessed May 26, 2021. https://johandemeij.com/music/profile/12.

Kierkegaard, Søren. "Journalen JJ:167." In *Søren Kierkegaards Skrifter*, edited by The Søren Kierkegaard Research Center. University of Copenhagen, 2012. Accessed June 9, 2021. http://sks.dk/forside/indhold.asp.

Magris, Claudio. *Danube: A Sentimental Journey from the Source to the Black Sea*. Translated by Patrick Creagh. New York: Farrar, Straus and Giroux, 2008.

Maslanka, David. "Program Note." Requiem. Maslanka Press. Last modified 2021. Accessed May 26, 2021. https://davidmaslanka.com/works/requiem-2013-11/.

Nolan, Christopher, dir. *Inception*. 2010; Burbank, CA: Warner Bros. Pictures.

Spielberg, Steven, dir. *Raiders of the Lost Ark*. 1981; Hollywood, CA: Paramount Pictures.

TEMPLE UNIVERSITY

Le Dressay, Alexis. *R.U.S.E.* Ubisoft. PC. 2010.

Merriam-Webster. s.v. "elegy (n.)." Accessed May 26, 2021. https://www.merriam-webster.com/dictionary/elegy.

Seeger, Pete. *Little Boxes.* Album: *Headlines and Footnotes: A Collection of Topical Songs.* 1999, originally recorded in 1963. Essex Music. Smithsonian Folkways Recordings. Streamed on Spotify.

Temple University. "Culture and History." Derry, Northern Ireland. Last modified 2018. Accessed May 29, 2021. https://studyabroad.temple.edu/sites/temple-summer-in-northern-ireland-irish-culture.

Theodore Presser Company. "Elegy for A Young American." Last modified 2021. Accessed May 26, 2021. https://www.presser.com/115-40083-elegy-for-a-young-american.html.

United States Marine Band. "LO PRESTI Elegy for a Young American – 'The President's Own' U.S. Marine Band." November 22, 2013. Video, 6:59. https://www.youtube.com/watch?v=BI2N8g7ouYw.

Westall, Mark. "TIME DECORATED: THE MUSICAL INFLUENCES OF JEAN-MICHEL BASQUIAT." *FAD Magazine,* January 15, 2021. Accessed June 11, 2021. https://fadmagazine.com/2021/01/15/time-decorated-the-musical-influences-of-jean-michel-basquiat/.

Young, Ralph. *Dissent: The History of an American Idea.* New York: New York University Press, 2015.

DERRY, NORTHERN IRELAND

Coulter, Phil and The Dubliners. *The Town I Loved So Well.* Album: *The Dubliners Compilation.* 2007, 4 discs. Originally recorded in 1973. Polydor Records Ltd. IML Irish Music Licensing Ltd. Streamed on Spotify.

Encyclopaedia Britannica. Online ed. s.v. "The Troubles: Northern Ireland history." Accessed May 30, 2021. https://www.britannica.com/event/The-Troubles-Northern-Ireland-history.

Fleming, Victor, dir. *The Wizard of Oz.* 1939; Beverly Hills, CA: Metro-Goldwyn-Mayer.

IrishCentral Staff. "What are the Eleventh Night bonfires in Northern Ireland?" *IrishCentral,* July 11, 2019. https://www.irishcentral.com/news/thenorth/what-are-eleventh-night-bonfires-northern-ireland.

ICE HOCKEY OFFICIATING

Piotrowski, Steve, Ty Halpin, and Marcia Stubbeman. *2018-2019 and 2019-2020 NCAA Men's and Women's Ice Hockey Rules and Interpretations.* Indianapolis: The National Collegiate Athletic Association, 2018.

Wolf, Dick. *Law & Order.* First aired September 13, 1990.

SHIFTING DIRECTION

Board of Regents of the University of Wisconsin System. "A Turning Point: Six Stories from The Dow Chemical Protests on Campus." Last modified 2019. Accessed May 31, 2021. https://1967.wisc.edu/.

Fulbright Austria (Austrian-American Educational Commission). "Live and teach English abroad in Austria." US Teaching Assistantships at Austrian Secondary Schools. Accessed May 27, 2021. https://www.usta-austria.at/site/home.

Institute of International Education, Inc. "Award Profile." 140 English Teaching Assistant Awards. Germany. Accessed May 27, 2021. https://us.fulbrightonline.org/countries/europe-and-eurasia/germany/148.

Kleiser, Randal, dir. *Grease*. 1978; Hollywood, CA: Paramount Pictures.

Seeger, Pete. *Waist Deep In The Big Muddy - Live*. Album: *Waist Deep In The Big Muddy and other Love Songs*. 1993, originally recorded in 1967. Columbia Records. Sony Music Entertainment Inc. Streamed on Spotify.

Swindoll, Charles. "Attitudes." The Value of a Positive Attitude. Insight for Today: A Daily Devotional by Pastor Chuck Swindoll. Charles R. Swindoll, Inc. Insight for Living Ministries. Published November 19, 2015. Last modified 2021. Accessed June 7, 2021. https://www.insight.org/resources/daily-devotional/individual/the-value-of-a-positive-attitude.

Temple University. "Diamond Peer Teachers Program." Last modified 2019. Accessed June 7, 2021. https://www.temple.edu/vpus/opportunities/peerteachers.html#:~:text=The%20Diamond%20Peer%20Teachers%20Program,and%20to%20provide%20supplemental%20instruction.

Temple University. "Program Description." Leipzig, Germany. Last modified 2018. Accessed May 27, 2021. https://studyabroad.temple.edu/sites/temple-summer-in-germany/program-description.

Williams, Roger. "The Bloudy Tenent of Persecution." In *Dissent in America: The Voices That Shaped a Nation*, by Ralph Young. Harlow: Longman Publishing Group, 2009.

Young, Ralph. *Dissent: The History of an American Idea*. New York: New York University Press, 2015.

Young, Ralph. *Dissent in America: The Voices That Shaped a Nation*. Harlow: Longman Publishing Group, 2009.

LEIPZIG, GERMANY

Encyclopaedia Britannica. Online ed. s.v. "Martin Luther: German religious leader." Accessed May 30, 2021. https://www.britannica.com/biography/Martin-Luther.

Encyclopaedia Britannica. Online ed. s.v. "Ninety-five Theses: work by Luther." Accessed May 30, 2021. https://www.britannica.com/event/Ninety-five-Theses.

Encyclopaedia Britannica. Online ed. s.v. "Protestantism." Accessed May 22, 2021. https://www.britannica.com/topic/Protestantism.

Gosenschenke "Ohne Bedenken." "Speisekarte." Accessed June 6, 2021. https://www. gosenschenke.de/speisekarte/.

National Geographic Society. "The Protestant Reformation." *National Geographic,* April 7, 2021. Accessed June 14, 2021. https://www.nationalgeographic.org/article/ protestant-reformation/.

Twain, Mark. *A Tramp Abroad.* Scotts Valley: CreateSpace Independent Publishing Platform, 2014.

Twain, Mark. *The Awful German Language.* Hamburg: Nikol Verlag, 2009.

Twain, Mark and Andreas Austilat. *A Tramp in Berlin: New Mark Twain Stories & an Account of Twain's Berlin Adventures.* New York: Berlinica, 2013.

THE YEAR LIKE NO OTHER

Galilei, Galileo. "Letter to the Grand Duchess Christina of Tuscany, 1615." In the *Modern History Sourcebook* and *International History Sourcebooks Project,* edited by the History Department of Fordham University and Paul Halsall. Last modified April 9, 2019. Accessed June 4, 2021. https://sourcebooks.fordham.edu/mod/galileo-tuscany.asp.

Magris, Claudio. *Danube: A Sentimental Journey from the Source to the Black Sea.* Translated by Patrick Creagh. New York: Farrar, Straus and Giroux, 2008.

Maslanka, David. "Program Note." Requiem. Maslanka Press. Last modified 2021. Accessed May 26, 2021. https://davidmaslanka.com/works/requiem-2013-11/.

Russo, Anthony and Joe Russo. *Avengers: Infinity War.* 2018; Burbank, CA: Marvel Studios.

Sinatra, Frank, singer. *September of My Years (Expanded Edition).* 2010, originally recorded in 1965. Reprise Records. Frank Sinatra Enterprises, LLC. Streamed on Spotify.

Whedon, Joss, dir. *Avengers: Age of Ultron.* 2015; Burbank, CA: Marvel Studios.